Form. a Limited Liability Company in Florida

Form a Limited Liability Company in Florida

Fourth Edition

Mark Warda

Attorney at Law

SPHINX® PUBLISHING
AN IMPRINT OF SOURCEBOOKS, INC.®
NAPERVILLE, ILLINOIS
www.SphinxLegal.com

Fourth Edition, 2007

Published by: **Sphinx® Publishing, A Division of Sourcebooks, Inc.®**

<u>Naperville Office</u>
P.O. Box 4410
Naperville, Illinois 60567-4410
630-961-3900
Fax: 630-961-2168
www.sourcebooks.com
www.SphinxLegal.com

This publication is designed to provide accurate and authoritative information in regard to the subject matter covered. It is sold with the understanding that the publisher is not engaged in rendering legal, accounting, or other professional service. If legal advice or other expert assistance is required, the services of a competent professional person should be sought.

From a Declaration of Principles Jointly Adopted by a Committee of the
American Bar Association and a Committee of Publishers and Associations

This product is not a substitute for legal advice.

Library of Congress Cataloging-in-Publication Data

Warda, Mark.
  Form a limited liability company in Florida / by Mark Warda. -- 4th ed.
    p. cm.
  Rev. ed. of: How to form a limited liability company in Florida. 3rd ed. 2005.
  ISBN-13: 978-1-57248-621-8 (pbk. : alk. paper)
  ISBN-10: 1-57248-621-X (pbk. : alk. paper) 1. Private companies--Florida--Popular works. 2. Limited partnership--Florida--Popular works. 3. Private companies--Florida--Forms. 4. Limited partnership--Florida--Forms.
I. Warda, Mark. How to form a limited liability company in Florida. II. Title.

KFF207.5.Z9W37 2007
346.759'0682--dc22

                              2007036462

Printed and bound in the United States of America.
SB — 10 9 8 7 6 5 4 3 2 1

Contents

Using Self-Help Law Books

Before using a self-help law book, you should realize the advantages and disadvantages of doing your own legal work and understand the challenges and diligence that this requires.

The Growing Trend

Rest assured that you will not be the first or only person handling your own legal matter. For example, in some states, more than 75% of the people in divorces and other cases represent themselves. Because of the high cost of legal services, this is a major trend, and many courts are struggling to make it easier for people to represent themselves. However, some courts are not happy with people who do not use attorneys and refuse to help them in any way. For some, the attitude is, "Go to the law library and figure it out for yourself."

We write and publish self-help law books to give people an alternative to the often complicated and confusing legal books found in most law libraries. We have made the explanations of the law as simple and easy to understand as possible. Of course, unlike an attorney advising an individual client, we cannot cover every conceivable possibility.

Cost/Value Analysis

Whenever you shop for a product or service, you are faced with various levels of quality and price. In deciding what product or service to buy, you make a cost/value analysis on the basis of your willingness to pay and the quality you desire.

When buying a car, you decide whether you want transportation, comfort, status, or sex appeal. Accordingly, you decide among choices such as a Neon, a Lincoln, a Rolls Royce, or a Porsche. Before making a decision, you usually weigh the merits of each option against the cost.

When you get a headache, you can take a pain reliever (such as aspirin) or visit a medical specialist for a neurological examination. Given this choice, most people, of course, take a pain reliever, since it costs only pennies; whereas a medical examination costs hundreds of dollars and takes a lot of time. This is usually a logical choice because it is rare to need anything more than a pain reliever for a headache. But in some cases, a headache may indicate a brain tumor, and failing to see a specialist right away can result in complications. Should everyone with a headache go to a specialist? Of course not, but people treating their own illnesses must realize that they are betting, on the basis of their cost/value analysis of the situation, that they are taking the most logical option.

The same cost/value analysis must be made when deciding to do one's own legal work. Many legal situations are very straightforward, requiring a simple form and no complicated analysis. Anyone with a little intelligence and a book of instructions can handle the matter without outside help.

But there is always the chance that complications are involved that only an attorney would notice. To simplify the law into a book like this, several legal cases often must be condensed into a single sentence or paragraph. Otherwise, the book would be several hundred pages long and too complicated for most people. However, this simplification necessarily leaves out many details and nuances that would apply to special or unusual situations. Also, there are many ways to interpret most legal questions. Your case may come before a judge who disagrees with the analysis of our authors.

Therefore, in deciding to use a self-help law book and to do your own legal work, you must realize that you are making a cost/value analysis. You have decided that the money you will save in doing it yourself outweighs the chance that your case will not turn out to your satisfaction. Most people handling their own simple legal matters never have a problem, but occasionally people find that it ended up costing them more to have an attorney straighten out the situation than it would have if they had hired an attorney in the beginning. Keep this in mind while handling your case, and be sure to consult an attorney if you feel you might need further guidance.

Local Rules

The next thing to remember is that a book which covers the law for the entire nation, or even for an entire state, cannot possibly include every procedural difference of every jurisdiction. Whenever possible, we provide the exact form needed; however, in some areas, each county, or even each judge, may require unique forms and procedures. In our state books, our forms usually cover the majority of counties in the state or provide examples of the type of form that will be required. In our national books, our forms are sometimes even more general in nature but are designed to give a good idea of the type of form that will be needed in most locations. Nonetheless, keep in mind that your state, county, or judge may have a requirement, or use a form, that is not included in this book.

You should not necessarily expect to be able to get all of the information and resources you need solely from within the pages of this book. This book will serve as your guide, giving you specific information whenever possible and helping you to find out what else you will need to know. This is just like if you decided to build your own backyard deck. You might purchase a book on how to build decks. However, such a book would not include the building codes and permit requirements of every city, town, county, and township in the nation; nor would it include the lumber, nails, saws, hammers, and other materials and tools you would need to actually build the deck. You would use the book as your guide, and then do some work and research involving such matters as whether you need a permit of some kind, what type and grade of wood is available in your area, whether to use hand tools or power tools, and how to use those tools.

Before using the forms in a book like this, you should check with your court clerk to see if there are any local rules of which you should be aware or local forms you will need to use. Often, such forms will require the same information as the forms in the book but are merely laid out differently or use slightly different language. They will sometimes require additional information.

Changes in the Law   Besides being subject to local rules and practices, the law is subject to change at any time. The courts and the legislatures of all fifty states are constantly revising the laws. It is possible that while you are reading this book, some aspect of the law is being changed.

In most cases, the change will be of minimal significance. A form will be redesigned, additional information will be required, or a waiting period will be extended. As a result, you might need to revise a form, file an extra form, or wait out a longer time period. These types of changes will not usually affect the outcome of your case. On the other hand, sometimes a major part of the law is changed, the entire law in a particular area is rewritten, or a case that was the basis of a central legal point is overruled. In such instances, your entire ability to pursue your case may be impaired.

Introduction

Each year over a hundred thousand new businesses are registered in Florida. Until recently, they have nearly all been corporations. In 1997, 109,063 new corporations were formed, but only 2,357 limited liability companies (LLCs). By 2006 the figures changed to 157,310 new corporations and 130,251 new LLCs.

The reason fewer LLCs were started earlier is that there was a 5.5% income tax that applied to all LLCs. Also, the start-up fees were higher for LLCs. But in 1998 and 1999, the LLC laws were changed drastically. The tax was eliminated, the fees lowered, and, perhaps best of all, interests in LLCs were protected from the claims of creditors. By 2006, the number of limited liability companies in Florida rose to 391,293. This number continues to increase every year.

Creating a basic limited liability company is not difficult. It is the purpose of this book to explain, in simple language, how you can do it yourself. As described in this book, a basic limited liability company is one in which all of the members are active in the business. Therefore, if you plan to have investors who are not active in the business, you should seek the advice of an attorney. The penalties for violation of securities laws are harsh. (see Chapter 6.)

The first three chapters explain the characteristics of LLCs. Chapters 4 and 5 explain how to set up and structure your LLC. Chapters 6, 7, 8, and 9 explain running, amending, and dissolving an LLC respectively.

If your situation is in any way complicated or involves factors not mentioned in this book, you should seek the advice of an attorney practicing business law. The cost of a short consultation can be a lot cheaper than the consequences of violating the law. Keep in mind, however, that the limited liability company is a new entity and few attorneys have much experience with them. The best attorney in this type of situation is one who promotes himself or herself as practicing in this particular area of business.

This book also explains the basics of taxation, but you should discuss your own particular situation with an accountant. He or she can also set you up with an efficient system of bookkeeping, which can save both time and money.

Good luck with your new business!

Limited Liability Company

A limited liability company is a relatively new invention of the law. For hundreds of years, the three choices of business entity were sole proprietorship, partnership, and corporation. However, the LLC was invented in 1977 by the state of Wyoming to fill a new need—businesses that wanted to be managed and taxed like partnerships, but protected from liability like a corporation. When the IRS acquiesced to this arrangement, every state in the union jumped on the bandwagon and passed laws allowing LLCs.

However, the laws passed were not identical. In some states, LLCs were very useful while in others they were practically useless. Florida's law fell into the useless category as it provided that LLCs were subject to the 5.5% corporate income tax that applies to *C corporations*. For most businesses, there was no reason to form an LLC when an *S corporation* offered exemption from the income tax. Florida also required LLCs to have two or more members, thus preventing sole proprietors from forming LLCs.

The law was amended in 1998 to exempt the LLC from the income tax and allow one-member LLCs. Suddenly, the number of LLCs being formed in Florida doubled. The law was amended again in 1999 to lower the fees for LLCs and to protect interests in LLCs from creditors' claims. The LLC is finally a very useful entity for Florida businesses. In many ways, it is a better choice for most small businesses than even an *S corporation* (a corporation in which the income is taxed to the shareholders, not the corporation).

Legally, an LLC is a legal person created under state law. As a person, an LLC has certain rights and obligations, such as the right to do business and the obligation to comply with the laws. Sometimes one hears of a law referring to natural persons. That is done in order to differentiate actual people from corporations and LLCs, which are legally created persons, but not natural persons.

The idea behind both the LLC and the corporation is to allow people to invest in a new business but not risk unlimited personal liability. Before the corporation was invented hundreds of years ago, people who invested in, say, an expedition to the New World to look for gold, could lose everything they owned in the event it went into debt. The invention of the corporation allowed people to put a limited sum of money into such a venture, split the profits if it succeeded, and not be liable if it failed.

The reasons for having a corporation or LLC are the same today. They allow investors to put up money for new ventures without risk of further liability. While our legal system is making more and more people liable for more and more things, legal entities such as the corporation and the LLC remain among the few innovations that have not yet been abandoned.

COMMON TERMS
Before forming an LLC, you should be familiar with these common terms used in the text.

Member   A *member* is a person who owns an interest in a limited liability company. It is similar to the stockholder of a corporation. However, unless the *Articles of Organization* provide otherwise, the members also manage the LLC. In this regard they are also similar to the directors or officers of a corporation.

Managing Member

A *managing member* is a member of the LLC who runs the operations. If all of the members do not want to manage the LLC, then one or more of them can be designated managing member.

Manager

A *manager* is a person who is not a member of the LLC but runs the business. This is sometimes done when the members of the LLC want a nonmember to run the operations or if they do not want their names listed on the secretary of state's website.

Registered Agent and Registered Office

The *registered agent* is the person designated by a limited liability company to receive legal papers that are served on the company. The registered agent should be regularly available at the registered office of the company. The registered office can be the company's offices, the office of the company's attorney, or the office of another person who is the registered agent. Technically, the registered office may not be a residence unless that address is also a business office of the limited liability company. The penalty for failing to comply with these rules could result in the dismissal of a lawsuit by a court and a fine of $5 per day (but not to exceed $500).

The registered agent is not an officer of the LLC who signs any papers for the LLC. Only the members or managers sign for the LLC. The registered agent only sits quietly waiting to receive court papers and forwards them to the members of the LLC.

Articles of Organization

The *Articles of Organization* is the document that is filed with the secretary of state to start the limited liability company. In most cases, it legally needs to contain only a few basic statements. Additional provisions can be added, but it is better in most cases to put such provisions in the membership agreement rather than the articles because amendment of the latter is more complicated.

Operating Agreement

The *operating agreement* is the document that includes the rules and regulations for the management of the company. Even single-member LLCs should have one, but they are especially important for multiple-member LLCs because they spell out the rights of the parties if they have a disagreement.

Before 1999, Florida statutes referred in several places to the regulations of the LLC. However, in 1999, all references to regulations were eliminated and replaced with operating agreement. If you have an existing LLC or come across a reference elsewhere to "regulations", this would apply to the operating agreement today.

Management Agreement   If the LLC is to be managed by less than all the members or by someone who is not a member, there should be a *management agreement* spelling out the rights and duties of the members and the managers.

Other Definitions   Legal definitions of other LLC terms are included in Florida Statutes (Fla. Stat.) Section (Sec.) 608.402 contained in Appendix A.

Advantages and Disadvantages

Before forming a limited liability company, the business owner or prospective business owner should become familiar with the advantages and disadvantages of the LLC and how they compare to those of other business entities.

COMPARED TO CORPORATIONS

LLCs are similar to corporations in that they allow you to start a business without worrying about unlimited liability. However, in creating the LLC, the legislature has given them some advantages over corporations.

Advantages   The main advantages that an LLC has over a corporation are as follows.

- ✪   The biggest advantage of an LLC over a corporation is that it provides double asset protection. A corporation provides asset protection in that a shareholder is protected from liabilities of the corporation. But a member of an LLC gets this protection plus his or her personal creditors cannot take his or her LLC away if set up correctly. This is explained in more detail in the next chapter.

✪ The fees are lower for an LLC than for a corporation. The startup fee of $125 is a little higher than the $70 for a corporation, but the annual fee is only $50 compared to $150 for a corporation. And if you forget to file your annual report on time, the penalty is $400 for a corporation but just $100 for an LLC.

✪ It is presumed by most legal experts that an LLC requires less formality than a corporation. While improper procedures in a corporation may allow a creditor to *pierce the corporate veil* and hold shareholders liable, the LLC is clearly meant to be a safe harbor to protect business owners from liability.

✪ An LLC can make special allocations of profits and losses among members, whereas S corporations cannot. S corporations must have one class of ownership in which profits and losses are allocated according to the percentage of ownership.

✪ In an LLC, money borrowed by the company can increase the tax basis of the owners and lower the taxes—in an S corporation, it does not.

✪ Contributing property to set up an LLC is not taxable, even for *minority interest owners*; whereas for a corporation, the Internal Revenue Code (IRC), Section 351 only allows it to be tax free for the contributors who have control of the business.

✪ The owners of an LLC can be foreign persons, other corporations, or any kind of trust, but the owners of corporations cannot be.

✪ An LLC may have an unlimited number of members, whereas an S corporation is limited to one hundred.

✪ If an S corporation violates one of the rules, it can lose its S corporation status and not be allowed to regain it for five years.

Another advantage may be mental hype. The LLC is a new entity and it may look more up-to-date to be an LLC than an ordinary corporation in the twenty-first century.

Disadvantages   The main disadvantage that most professionals see in the LLC is that the law is new and it is not yet known how the courts will interpret it. But for some lawyers this is an excuse not to learn new things. It is always more comfortable to do what you have always done.

While there is always a chance for bad interpretation of the law, most cases should turn out as the law intended. The LLC law was modeled after the limited partnership law. In a case against the famous (or infamous) Charles Givens, a creditor convinced the trial judge to let it seize Givens' limited partnership interest. The appeals court reversed that judgment saying:

> *We believe the statute means what it says: the Florida Revised Uniform Limited Partnership Act specifically gives a judgment creditor the rights of an assignee— nothing more. Accordingly, the order of the trial court is reversed with instructions to follow section 620.153 of the Florida Revised Uniform Limited Partnership Act.*
>
> (*Givens v. National Loan Investors, LP,* 724 So.2d 610 (Fla. Dist. 5, 1998).)

Because of the similarity between LLCs and LPs, there is a good chance that a future court will rule the same way on the LLC statute.

For the LLC that is disregarded for tax purposes, there can be the disadvantage that all earned income is subject to the self-employment tax, unlike in an S corporation in which some money can be taken out as salary and some as dividends. However, the LLC can opt to be taxed as a corporation and then opt to be taxed as an S corporation.

For a large business in which the owners take out salaries of $85,000 or more plus profits, there would not be much difference since the Social Security tax does not apply above that level. But for a smaller business, in which an owner would take out say, $30,000 salary and $20,000 profit, the extra taxes on the $20,000 would be over $3,000. If this is an issue, then you can still have an LLC, but you can opt to be taxed as a corporation, and then file **IRS FORM 2553** (form 8, p.165) to be treated as an S corporation.

According to a 2007 court case, the owners of an LLC that is taxed as a disregarded entity like a partnership or proprietorship can be personally liable for payroll taxes that are not paid by the company. Shareholders of a corporation would not be liable for these taxes if they were not officers or directors.

COMPARED TO LIMITED PARTNERSHIPS

A *limited partnership* (LP) is an entity in which one or more partners control the business and are liable for the debts (the *general partners*); and one or more partners have an investment in the business, but no say in its management nor liability for the debts (the *limited partners*).

Advantages of an LLC

The advantages of a limited liability company over a limited partnership are as follows.

○ The LLC offers more protection from liability because it does not need a general partner.

○ The formation and annual fees of an LLC are lower than for a limited partnership.

○ The legal fees for setting up an LLC are much cheaper because the paperwork is much simpler.

○ An LLC may have one member but a limited partnership may not.

○ An LLC has some tax advantages, such as allowing passive losses and increases in the tax basis, which give the members more tax deductions.

Advantages of an LP

The advantages of a limited partnership over an LLC are as follows.

○ Some argue that the longer history of the limited partnership offers more legal precedent for court cases that may come up.

○ Profits of an LLC are more likely to be subject to the Social Security and Medicare taxes than limited partnership interests. (However, the issue has not been completely settled by the courts.)

COMPARED TO PARTNERSHIPS AND PROPRIETORSHIPS

The limited liability company offers the greatest benefits when compared to *partnerships* and *sole proprietorships*. Now that the LLC structure is available, it is foolish for most partnerships and sole proprietorships not to switch.

Advantages of an LLC

Limited liability. The main reason for forming a limited liability company or corporation is to limit the liability of the owners. In a sole proprietorship or partnership, the owners are personally liable for the debts and liabilities of the business. Also, creditors are able to go after all of their assets (business and personal) to collect. If an LLC is formed and operated properly, the owners can be protected from all such liability.

Example 1:

If several people are in a partnership and one of them makes many large, extravagant purchases in the name of the partnership, the other partners can be held liable for the full amount of all such purchases. The creditors can take the bank accounts, cars, real estate, and other property of any partner to pay the debts of the partnership. If only one partner has money, he or she may have to pay all of the debts accumulated by all the other partners. When doing business in the LLC form, the company may go bankrupt and the shareholders may lose their initial investment, but the creditors cannot touch the assets of the owners.

Example 2:

If a person runs a taxi business and one of the drivers causes a terrible accident, the owner can be held liable for the full amount of the damages. If the taxi driver was on drugs, killed several people, and the damages amount to millions of dollars more than the insurance coverage, the owner may lose everything he or she owns. With a corporation or LLC, only the business would be liable and if there was not enough money, the owner still could not be touched.

One true story involved a business owner who owned hundreds of taxis. He put one or two in each of hundreds of different corporations that he owned. Each corporation only had minimum insurance and when one taxi was involved in an accident, the owner only lost the assets of that corporation. The injured party tried to reach the owner's other assets, but the court ruled that this was a valid use of the corporate structure.

NOTE: *If a member of a limited liability company does something negligent, signs a debt personally, or guarantees a company debt, the limited liability company will not protect him or her from the consequences of his or her own act or from the debt.*

Also, if a limited liability company does not follow the proper formalities, it may be ignored by a court and the owners or officers may be held personally liable. The formalities include having separate bank accounts, filing annual reports, and following other requirements of state law.

There have been only a few cases interpreting the law because the limited liability company is relatively new. Courts will most likely look to both corporation and partnership law when ruling in a limited liability company case. When a court ignores a corporate structure and holds the owners or officers liable, it is called *piercing the corporate veil*. It is not yet clear how or when the courts would allow a party to pierce the LLC structure. (A clear explanation of Florida law on piercing the corporate veil is contained in the Florida Supreme Court case, *Dania Jai-Alai Palace, Inc. v. Sykes,* 450 So.2d 1114 (1984).)

Continuous existence. A limited liability company may have a perpetual existence. When a sole proprietor or partner dies, the assets of his or her business may go to his or her heirs, but the business no longer exists. If the surviving spouse or other heirs of a business owner want to continue the business in their own names, they will be considered a new business—even if they are using the assets of the old business. With a partnership, the death of one partner may cause a *dissolution* of the business.

Example 1:

If a person dies owning a sole proprietorship, his or her spouse may want to continue the business. That person may inherit all of the assets, but will have to start a new business. This means getting new licenses and tax numbers, registering the name, and establishing credit from scratch. With an LLC, the business continues with all of the same licenses, bank accounts, etc.

Example 2:

If one partner dies, the partnership may be forced out of business. The heirs of the deceased partner can force the sale of his or her share of the assets of the partnership, even if surviving partners need them to continue the business. If the surviving partners do not have the money to buy out the heirs, the business may have to be dissolved. With an LLC, the heirs would only inherit membership interest. With properly drawn documents, the business could continue.

Ease of transferability. A limited liability company and all of its assets and accounts may be transferred by the simple assignment of an *interest* (stake) in the company. With a sole proprietorship, each of the individual assets must be transferred and the accounts, licenses, and permits must be individually transferred.

Example:

Jack sold his sole proprietorship to Kim. Kim, as the new owner, will have to get a new occupational license, set up her own bank account, and apply for a new taxpayer identification number. The title to any vehicles and real estate will have to be put in her name. Also, all open accounts will have to be changed to her name. She will probably have to submit new credit applications. With an LLC, all of these items remain in the same company name. As the new member, the new owner would elect him- or herself or any other person as LLC manager.

NOTE: *In some cases, the new owners will have to submit personal applications for such things as credit lines or liquor licenses, because these are granted to the owners of the company, not to the company.*

Sharing ownership. With a limited liability company, the owner of a business can share the profits of a business without giving up control. This is done by setting up the share of profits separate from the share of ownership.

Example:

If a person wants to give her children some of the profits of her business, she can make them members of the company, entitling them to a share of the profits but not giving them any control over management of the company. This would not be practical with a sole proprietorship or partnership.

Ease of raising capital. A limited liability company may raise capital by admitting new members or borrowing money. In most cases, a business does not pay taxes on money it raises by the sale of its shares.

Example:

If an LLC or corporation wants to expand, the owners can sell off ten percent, fifty percent, or ninety percent of the owner-ship and still remain in control of the business. The people putting up the money may be more willing to invest if they know they will have a piece of the action than if they were making a loan with a limited return. They may not want to become partners in a partnership.

NOTE: *There are strict rules about selling interests in businesses with criminal penalties and triple damages for violators. (see Chapter 6.)*

Separate record-keeping. An LLC has all its own bank accounts and records. A partner or sole proprietor may have trouble differentiating which of his or her expenses were for business and which were for personal items.

Ease of estate planning. With an LLC or corporation, shares of a company can be distributed more easily than with a partnership or sole proprietorship. Different heirs can be given different percentages and control can be limited to those who are most capable. This is done by having different classes of ownership, different distribution of profits, and different levels of control.

Example:
A person owning an LLC who wants to leave it to three children could set it up so that only the child with the good business judgment becomes the company manager, and the child who is handicapped gets a larger percentage of the profits.

Also, under Florida's Transfer on Death law, the membership interests can be set up to pass automatically at death. A husband and wife owning an LLC together can each own 50% and specify that his or her share should *transfer on death* to the other and in the event of both of their deaths it would go to their children.

Death taxes can be avoided if small amounts of ownership are transferred tax free each year before death. But for this you should consult a tax expert because the IRS rules must be followed carefully.

Prestige. The name of an LLC or corporation sounds more prestigious than the name of a sole proprietor to some people. John Smith d/b/a Acme Builders sounds like one lone guy. Acme Builders, LLC, sounds like it might be a large, sophisticated operation. No one needs to know that it is run out of a garage.

Separate credit rating. An LLC has its own credit rating, which can be better or worse than the owner's credit rating. An LLC can go bankrupt while the owner's credit remains unaffected, or an owner's credit may be bad but the corporation may maintain a good rating.

Disadvantages of an LLC

The LLC does have some disadvantages that should be weighed against the advantages.

Cost. Compared to a sole proprietorship or partnership, an LLC is a little more expensive to operate. There is a registration fee of $125 and an annual fee of $50. The start-up cost is only slightly more than for a corporation, but proprietorships and general partnerships do not have start-up or annual fees.

Taxes. A limited liability company owner will have to pay unemployment compensation for him- or herself, which he or she would not have to pay as a sole proprietor. The state unemployment tax starts at 2.7% of the first $7,000 ($189 per year). If there are no claims it drops to 0.12% of $7,000 ($8.40 per year).

Banking. Checks made out to a limited liability company cannot be cashed; they must be deposited into a corporate account. Some banks have higher fees just for businesses that are incorporated. (See page 43 for tips on avoiding high bank fees.)

Separate records. The owners of a limited liability company must be careful to keep their personal business separate from the business of the limited liability company. The limited liability company must have its own records and should have minutes of meetings. Money must be kept separate. Records should be separate in every business and the structure of a company might make it easier to do so.

Appearance in court. While an individual is allowed to appear in court without hiring an attorney, an LLC—like a corporation or partnership—is required to hire an attorney to appear in court. In one case, a bankruptcy filed by a manager of an LLC was thrown out and he was accused of practicing law without a license.

CONVERTING AN EXISTING BUSINESS

Because of the benefits afforded by LLCs, it would be worthwhile converting most proprietorships and partnerships to LLCs. Corporations are more complicated, but the conversion may be worthwhile for those concerned with asset protection.

By converting a business, rather than forming a new one, you can save some time because you will keep your same employer identification number, state tax number, and many others.

For entities that are not corporations, a **CERTIFICATE OF CONVERSION** should be filed. (see form 4, p.151.) Corporations cannot merely convert, but must be merged into a new LLC or sell its assets to a new LLC. Because of the possible tax consequences, if you have an existing corporation, seek expert tax advice before converting to an LLC.

BUSINESS COMPARISON CHART

	Sole Proprietorship	General Partnership	Limited Partnership	Limited Liability Co.	Corporation C or S	Nonprofit Corporation
Liability Protection	No	No	For limited partners	For all members	For all shareholders	For all members
Taxes	Pass through	Pass through	Pass through	Pass through of corporate	S corps. pass through C corps. pay tax	None on income Employees pay on wages
Minimum # of Members	1	2	2	1	1	3
Start-up Fee	None	$50 optional	$35 plus $7 per $1000 Min. $87.50 Max. $1,855	$125	$70	$70
Annual Fee	None	$25 optional	$103.75 plus $7 per $1000 Min. $156.25 Max. $676.25	$50	$150	$61.25
Diff. Classes of Ownership	No	Yes	Yes	Yes	S corps. No C corps. Yes	No ownership Diff. classes of membership
Survives after Death	No	No	Yes	Yes	Yes	Yes
Best for	1 person Low-risk business or no assets	Low-risk business	Low-risk business with silent partners	All types of businesses	All types of businesses	Charitable Educational

Asset Protection

The main reason for having an LLC is to limit liability. Because the asset protection advantages of an LLC are so much greater than other entities and the fees and paperwork are both lower, the LLC is the entity of choice for nearly any type of business. Many people are setting up multiple LLCs just for asset protection for each of their different assets.

DOUBLE ASSET PROTECTION

The really great thing about the LLC is that it offers two types of asset protection. One is the same as a corporation; the other is the same as a limited partnership. Together these make the LLC one of the most valuable asset protection tools that exists.

Corporate-Type Protection
A corporation protects its owners from liability in that the shareholders are protected from the debts and liabilities of the business. If you own stock in General Motors, you will not be liable if they default on their bonds or if someone sues General Motors for defective cars and wins billions of dollars.

This same type of protection is available to you if you own a corporation (S corporation or C corporation) or an LLC. If the company is liable for something (and you did not personally cause it) then you as the shareholder or member will in most cases not be liable.

Limited Partnership-Type Protection

With an LLC you get an additional type of asset protection not afforded to corporations. Under Florida's LLC law, if you do something personally that makes you liable—for example, you get into an auto accident—the creditor cannot take your LLC assets away from you. What the law says is that your creditor can only get a *charging order* against your interest. This means that he or she cannot take ownership of your interest in the LLC or liquidate the assets of the LLC. The only thing the creditor can do is pay the taxes on your share of the LLC profits (even if no profits are distributed). No profits need to be distributed unless the other member (your spouse, for example) decides to distribute them. Needless to say, most creditors do not want to get charging orders. Sometimes they will settle their claim for pennies on the dollar instead.

Any assets you put into an LLC can be safe from creditors, no matter what you do—malpractice, auto accidents, divorce, bankruptcy. A creditor can take your General Motors stock and your S corporation stock, but not your LLC interest. But note the verb *can*. In law, nothing is black and white, and new law is an especially gray area. But if you follow the rules you can be successful.

REQUIREMENTS FOR DOUBLE ASSET PROTECTION

While the law says that a creditor can only have a charging order against an LLC interest, at least one court has ruled that if the LLC has only one member the creditor can take the company. The rationale was that the charging order rule was designed to protect other members of a business from disruption from one member's creditors, and this does not make sense in a one-member company. This was not a Florida case but is the only case discussing this important issue. Florida courts could rule differently, but they could decide to follow this case. This means that you probably need at least two members in your LLC to get the double asset protection.

Entrepreneurs who do not really want someone else in their business look for ways to have a two-member company but to still keep full control. Some of the suggestions have been to have part of the LLC owned by:

- ❂ a corporation owned by the member;

- ❂ another LLC owned by the member;

- ❂ a trust owned by the member;

- ❂ a child; or,

- ❂ a parent.

Will these work? If the one member really controls 100% then probably not. Courts usually look to the substance of the whole transaction to see what the reality is. If you just assign 2% of your LLC to your corporation simply to avoid creditors, it will probably be considered a sham transaction.

What would work is a setup with some purpose. If your parent made a small investment in your business in exchange for a small percentage of ownership, that would be legitimate. If you set up a trust for your children's education and it bought a part of your LLC, that would probably also be seen as legitimate.

Example:
A doctor sold a small percentage of his LLC to his accountant. If this appeared to be a plan to share profits in exchange for services, rather than merely a pretense, it might work.

One thing to consider is that the success of a plan depends on the sophistication of the creditor. While a thorough examination by a sophisticated creditor's attorney could make any plan look suspect, if a new attorney is faced with multiple LLCs and a complicated setup that could take months to decipher, he or she might be willing to accept your settlement offer or insurance limits, rather than spend the time to try to get through it.

The fact that this is a gray area of law works two ways. For the person wanting to protect him- or herself, it does not give clear answers on what works best. For the creditor, it does not provide how it can win. No matter what type of LLC arrangement you have set up, if a creditor wins against you, you can appeal it and argue that the law gives you more protection. Plaintiff's lawyers do not like to spend years in court unless there is a real big payoff. A small business with a complicated structure and no sure legal basis would be a good candidate for a quick settlement.

Executory Contract

Some have argued that even though Florida law provides that a charging order is the only remedy for a creditor, a bankruptcy court could seize a person's interest. No Florida bankruptcy court has ruled on this theory, but an Arizona bankruptcy court ruled that when the LLC agreement is an *executory contract* (both sides have obligations), then the interest is protected by state law.

This means that the more obligations that a member has, the safer his or her interest is from creditors. Some possible obligations are contributing capital when needed, participating in the management, and attending meetings. In some LLC arrangements a member might not want to be required to add more capital, but one would need to weigh the risks and decide whether putting too much money in the LLC or losing the LLC to creditors was a greater risk.

If one were dealing with strangers one would not want to be obligated to add more money, but if it was a family-held business protection from creditors would be a greater risk, and the worry of being required to add capital would be nil.

WHEN TO USE A SINGLE-MEMBER COMPANY

While a single-member LLC does not provide double asset protection, it can still be very useful in many situations. Remember, a single-member LLC protects the owner against business claims but does not protect the business from the member's creditors. So the best use occurs when the business would have claims, but the company does not have many assets worth claiming.

A good example is a property management company. Many real estate investors have one LLC set up to manage their properties. Usually it will collect the rents and pay the mortgages and expenses of the properties. This company deals with the tenants and has a high risk of getting sued. But if it spends all the money it collects in rents it will not have many assets so it does not need double asset protection.

Another use could be to own individual properties. If you have one LLC that owns five properties then a liability on one property could cause you to lose them all. A better plan would be to have each property in a separate single-member LLC all owned by one multiple-member LLC. The single-member LLCs would not file tax returns, but would pass through their income to the multiple-member LLC.

The chart on page 22 demonstrates how multiple LLCs can be used to hold investments, as well as when tax returns would need to be filed, based on whether it was a single-member company or a multiple-member LLC.

(Thanks to David Burton, CPA, of Harper Van Skoik & Co., Clearwater, for this planning.)

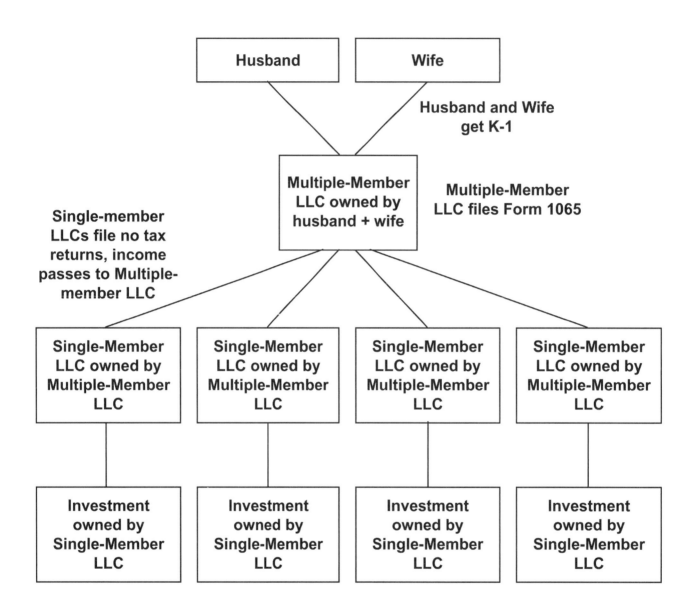

Types of LLCs

chapter 4

Before forming your LLC, you need to decide which type of LLC it will be:

- ✪ Florida or foreign;

- ✪ member-managed or manager-managed;

- ✪ single-member or multi-member; and,

- ✪ whether it will be a professional LLC.

FLORIDA LLC OR FOREIGN LLC

The previous chapters discussed LLCs in general and specific advantages of a Florida-based LLC. However, a person wishing to form a limited liability company must decide whether the company will be a Florida company or a *foreign company*. A foreign limited liability company is one formed in another state that does business in Florida. Two states that have been recognized as being favorable to business are Delaware and Nevada.

Delaware LLCs In the past, there was some advantage to forming a business in Delaware, since that state had very liberal business laws and a long history of court decisions favorable to businesses. Many national corporations are formed there for these reasons. However, Florida has liberalized its LLC laws and today has most of the same advantages as Delaware, including no income tax and low filing fees. So the only reason to choose Delaware would be if you planned to soon be listed on a national stock exchange with shareholders throughout the country.

Nevada LLCs Nevada has liberalized its business laws recently to attract companies to the state. It has low filing fees, allows more privacy and other benefits depending on the type of entity, and it does not have a state income tax. This is why people in many states prefer to start their companies in Nevada. However, Florida also has no income tax, even lower fees for LLCs, and does not disclose any more information on its website. So Florida businesses would not have an advantage in Florida.

Series LLCs In some states it is possible to form series LLCs, which are single limited liability companies that can segregate assets into separate subentities so that liability can be limited to single assets. States that currently allow these are Delaware, Illinois, Iowa, Nevada, Oklahoma, Oregon, Tennessee, and Utah, but other states may allow them in the near future.

The main benefit of the series LLC is to lower the filing fees for people who have many assets. In some states the annual fees are hundreds or thousands of dollars a year for a single LLC. Since Florida's annual fee is only $50, starting a series LLC in another state would probably not be much of a benefit and the costs of complying with the out-of-state laws might be greater than the Florida fees. If Florida begins to allow series LLCs to be formed here then they might be more attractive entities.

Disadvantages The biggest disadvantage to forming a business in Nevada, Delaware, or any other state is that you will need to have an agent, an office, or both in that state You will also have to register as a foreign LLC doing business in Florida. This is more expensive and more complicated than just forming your company in Florida. Also, if you are sued by someone who is not in Florida, they can sue you in the state in which you were formed. This would probably be more expensive for you than a suit filed in your local court. Additionally, if you incorporate in a state that has an income tax, you may have to pay taxes there even if you only do business in Florida.

MEMBER-MANAGED OR MANAGER-MANAGED

The next thing you will need to decide is whether your LLC will be member-managed or manager-managed. The question is whether all the members will have an equal control of the company's business or whether there will be one or more people who control the business while the others are mostly silent.

Member-Managed

If the LLC is being formed by one person or a small number of people who will operate as equal partners, you should be a member-managed company. In this case you would use the LIMITED LIABILITY COMPANY MEMBER-MANAGED OPERATING AGREEMENT. (see form 10, p.169.) This form is explained in the next chapter.

Manager-Managed

If the LLC will have one or more persons who will make all the business decisions and members who are not active in the business except to put up money, then you should form a manager-managed LLC. In this case, you would use the LIMITED LIABILITY COMPANY MANAGEMENT OPERATING AGREEMENT. (see form 11, p.173.) This form is explained in the next chapter. Be sure to read about securities laws in Chapter 6 if you have a manager-managed company.

SINGLE-MEMBER OR MULTIPLE-MEMBER

Whether you use a single-member or multiple-member LLC is not just a function of the number of people involved. Because of the advantages and disadvantages of each, a single business owner might want to form a multiple-member company and multiple people might want to form single-member companies.

For example, a person with a one-person business who wants to start a multiple-member LLC to gain asset protection, might want to make his spouse, parent, or child a member. Two people who own several properties as separate LLCs might want to make them single-member LLCs owned by one multiple-member LLC to avoid filing a separate tax return for each. (See chart on page 22 for a breakdown of tax returns filed.)

You will have an operating agreement whether you are a single- or multiple-member company. But for a multiple-member company, you need to be more careful to spell out each others' rights in the event of a split-up, death, or an irreconcilable disagreement.

Taxes   A single-member LLC is easier for tax purposes because no tax return is required. The income is reported on the member's tax return. A multiple member LLC must file IRS Form 1065, the partnership tax return, and give the members K-1 forms to file with their returns. If you do your own taxes this may be just another form to file, but if you have a professional tax preparer, it may cost hundreds of dollars. If you set up numerous LLCs this can get expensive.

Asset Protection   While a single-member LLC is simpler for tax purposes, it probably will not be allowed double asset protection. As explained in Chapter 3, you need two or more members for the double asset protection that an LLC offers. Therefore, if your LLC will have substantial assets it should be set up as multiple-member to obtain asset protection.

REGULAR OR PROFESSIONAL LLC

Certain types of services can only be rendered by a limited liability company if it is a *professional limited liability company* (PLLC). These are such services as performed by attorneys, physicians, certified public accountants, veterinarians, architects, life insurance agents, chiropractors, and similarly licensed businesses. A professional limited liability company must comply with all the rules of a regular limited liability company, found in Florida Statutes, Chapter 608, unless they conflict with Chapter 621, which specifically governs professional service corporations and limited liability companies. The major differences between the two are as follows.

✪   A professional limited liability company must have one specific purpose spelled out in the **ARTICLES OF ORGANIZATION** and that purpose must be to practice one of the professions. It may not

engage in any other business, but it may invest its funds in real estate, stocks, bonds, mortgages, or other types of investments. A professional service company may change its purpose to another legal purpose, but it will then no longer be a professional service limited liability company.
(Fla. Stat. Secs. 621.05 and 621.08.)

✪ The name of a professional limited liability company must contain the word *chartered, professional limited company,* or the abbreviation *P.L.C.* It may use its name without these words if it registers for a fictitious name. A professional limited liability company may not use only *company*, or the words *corporation*, *incorporated*, or any abbreviation of these. It may contain the name of some or all of the shareholders and may contain the names of deceased or retired shareholders.
(Fla. Stat. Sec. 621.12.)

✪ Only persons licensed to practice the profession may be members of a professional limited liability company. A member who loses his or her right to practice must immediately sever all employment with, and financial interests in, such company. If such a shareholder does not, the company may be dissolved by the Florida Department of Legal Affairs. No member may enter into a voting trust or other similar arrangement with anyone.
(Fla. Stat. Secs. 621.09, 621.10, and 621.11.)

✪ A professional limited liability company may not merge with any other limited liability company, except a Florida professional service corporation or professional limited liability company that is licensed to perform the same type of services. (Fla. Stat. Sec. 621.051.)

Start-Up Procedures

This chapter explains all the steps you need to follow to form your own Florida limited liability company.

CHOOSING THE COMPANY NAME

The very first thing to do before starting a limited liability company is to thoroughly research the name you wish to use in order to be sure it is available. Many businesses have been forced to stop using their name after spending thousands of dollars promoting it.

Florida Records The first place to check on the availability of a name is the Florida Department of State's website. If someone already has the name you want, your filing will be rejected. Their searchsite is currently located at:

www.sunbiz.org/corinam.html

The screen will look like this:

Just type in the name you want to use (or any name you want to search) and hit the "Search Now" button. (For this example, the name *ABC Enterprises* was used.) You will then get a list like this:

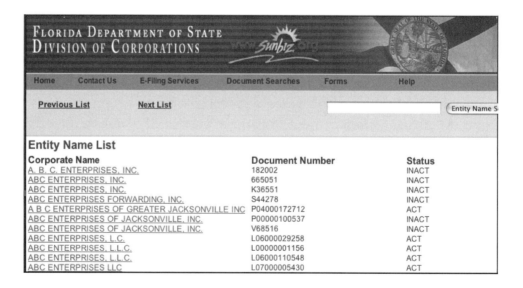

Fictitious Names

You can see that there are many companies with similar names. But if you look at the right-hand column, you will see that only one is active. You would be allowed to take the name of an inactive company, but it would not be a good idea. If the inactive company had creditors, there might be some confusion and they might go after you. If the inactive business was closed decades ago and was located in another part of the state, it would be less dangerous to take the name but you would always be better off changing the name slightly.

Fictitious names are names registered by businesses that are not the name of the company itself. You can and should check these online on the department of state website at:

www.sunbiz.org/ficinam.html

The search screen will look like this:

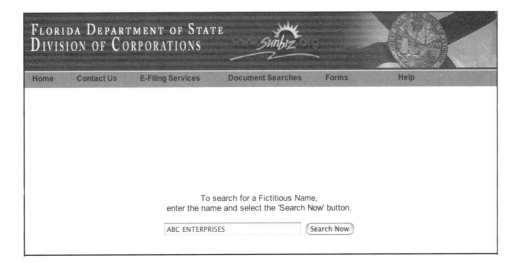

And the results will look like this:

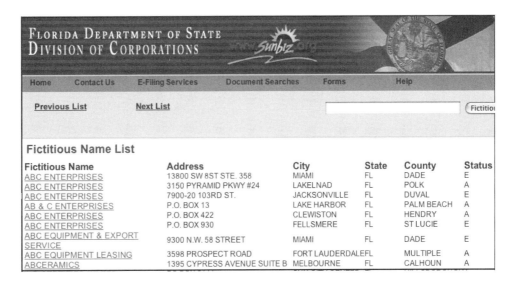

If someone else has a fictitious name that is the same as the business name you want to use, you might want to consider another name. While the secretary of state will allow you to file with the same name as a fictitious name, the fictitious name owner might have some legal rights to the name and might sue you for taking it as your own. If the business is far from the area where your business is located, there would be less risk of confusion and thus less risk of a suit, but it is always better to have a name completely different from other businesses.

When forming a new company, you will probably not need a fictitious name yourself. Your company's name will probably be your business name. Some examples of when a fictitious name may be needed include:

❂   if a person who names his or her company something like John Smith, LLC, he or she might want to use the fictitious name Smith Family Realty, or

❂   if the company has a common name like Jones Flooring, LLC, it might want to add a location and use a fictitious name such as Jones Flooring of Miami, Jones Flooring of Key West, etc.

Florida Trademarks   If someone has a Florida trademark on a name, you will not be able to use it. Therefore, you need to check the Division of Corporations' trademark records as well. Search its site at:

www.sunbiz.org/coritm.html

The screen that appears will look like this:

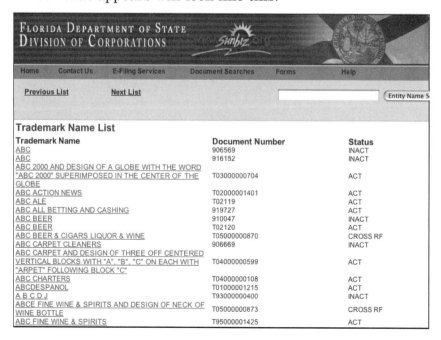

Federal Trademarks

While there may be a lot of businesses around the country using names similar to what you want to use that will not cause you problems, if they have registered a federal trademark of the name, they can force you to stop using it and you could be liable for damages. So it is best to check the trademarks registered with the United States Patent and Trademark Office (USPTO).

Trademark Records Search. Up until 1999, the only ways to search the records of the United States Patent and Trademark Office were to go there, use a Trademark Depository Library, or hire a search firm to do a search. But now you can do a search instantly on the Internet. The website is **www.uspto.gov**. Once there click on "Search TM database (TESS)" under "Trademarks" on the left side of the screen. Here is what you will see:

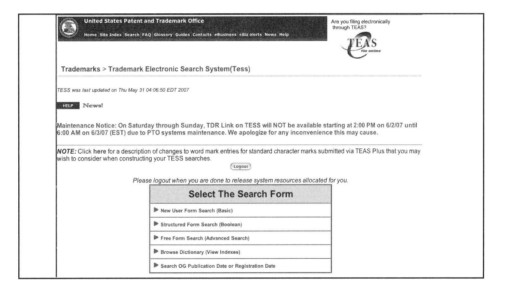

The database is updated regularly, but it is usually a few weeks behind schedule. You will see the date it is current through in the first paragraph. Clicking on the "News!" button will give you the latest complete filing date available online from the USPTO. As a practical matter, if a mark you are considering has not been registered in the last two hundred years, it is not likely that it has been in the last few weeks, but it is possible, especially if you are using a mark related to the latest technology. If you wish to update your mark through the latest filings, you will need to either visit the USPTO or hire a search firm to do so.

Unregistered Names

Even if a business does not register its name, it still has legal rights to it. Therefore you should check to see if any other businesses have the name you intend to use. If a business in your area has a similar name you should not use it. If the business is farther away, you can use it if you do not expect to do business in that area, but still, a completely different name is better.

For a thorough search you can use the Internet search engine Google or Yahoo, but you may find more listings than you can ever look at. (A search of "Sphinx" returns over a million references.) If you go to a *white pages* listing of business names you will get a more limited list. One site that lets you search all states at once is **www.switchboard.com**.

Similar Names
Sometimes it seems like every good name is taken. But a name can often be modified slightly or used on a different type of goods or services. If there is a "TriCounty Painting, L.L.C." in Pensacola, it may be possible to use something like "TriCounty Painting of Tampa Bay, L.L.C.," if you are in a different part of the state. Try different variations if your favorite name is taken. However, keep in mind that if you eventually expand your business to an area where the name is used, you can be barred from using a name if someone else has already established it there. In such a case, you would have been better off starting your business with a completely different name.

Another possibility is to give the corporation one name and do business under a fictitious name. (See "Fictitious Names" on page 31.)

Example:
If you want to use the name "Flowers by Freida" in Miami and there is already a "Flowers by Freida, Inc." in Pensacola, you might register your company under the name "Freida Jones, L.L.C." Then, register the company as doing business under the fictitious name "Flowers by Freida." Unless "Flowers by Freida, Inc." has registered a trademark for the name either in Florida or nationally, you will probably be able to use the name.

NOTE: *You should realize that you might run into complications later, especially if you decide to expand into other areas of the state. One protection available would be to register the name as a trademark. This would give you exclusive use of the name anywhere that someone else was not already using it.*

Name Requirements

The limited liability company name must contain one of the following at the end of the name.

LLC   L.L.C.   limited liability company

NOTE: *Until December 31, 2007, an LLC can be registered using "LC," "L.L.C.," or "limited company" in the name, but beginning January 1, 2008, those will not be allowed for new companies.*

The word limited can be abbreviated "Ltd." and the word company can be abbreviated "Co."

A person who knowingly leaves one of these endings off of an LLC's name, or agrees to the omission, can be personally liable for any indebtedness, damage, or liability caused by the omission.

The name cannot include any words implying that it is part of the state or federal government, or that it is a part of any business in which it is not authorized to be.

A professional LLC must use the word *chartered*, the words *professional limited company*, or the abbreviation *P.L.* as part of its company name, but it can leave this off of its fictitious name if it has registered one.

Forbidden Names

A limited liability company may not use certain words in its name if there would be a likelihood of confusion. There are state and federal laws that control the use of these words. In most cases, your application will be rejected if you use a forbidden word. Some of the words that may not be used without special licenses or registration are:

Assurance	Insurance
Banc	Lottery
Bank	Olympiad
Banker	Olympic
Banking	Savings Bank
College	Savings and Loan Association
Cooperative	Spaceport Florida
Credit Union	Trust Company
Disney	University
Florida Spaceport	

ARTICLES OF ORGANIZATION

The act that creates the LLC is the filing of *Articles of Organization*. This can be a paper copy sent to Tallahassee, or an electronic copy filed online.

To begin your online filing, go to **www.sunbiz.org/index.html,** click "Electronic Filing", at which point you will get this screen:

Select "FL Limited Liability Company Articles of Organization" from the drop-down menu and click the "Add Filing" button after checking the box next to the statement saying you have read and accept the disclaimer. You will get a long page that begins like this:

The data should be completed as follows.

✪ No *effective date* is needed unless you want the company to start at some specific date other than the filing date. It can be five days in the past or between ninety days in the future.

✪ If you want one or more *Certificate of Status* or *Certified Copy* you can select the quantity. The costs are $30 for a Certified Copy and $5 for a Certificate of Status. (Usually you do not need these copies.)

✪ Next, type in the exact *name* of the company you are starting.

✪ The *principle place of business* can be any place, even outside the state of Florida, but it cannot be a post office box.

✪ If you prefer to use a post office box or other *mailing address* different from your physical address, it can be listed.

✪ The *registered agent* is the person designated by the company to receive legal papers on behalf of the company. A registered agent must have a street address and must sign the acceptance of appointment to the position. This is done electronically by typing the agent's name in the form.

✪ For *Limited Liability Purpose* you should check the box "Any lawful purpose." If you were to type in, for example, "lawn service" then your business could not later decide to handle house painting without amending its Articles of Organization. It is better to leave it unlimited. (For professional limited liability companies, see p.26.)

✪ *Correspondence name and email address* is the person the division will email with the confirmation and any questions.

✪ *Signature* can be a member or any person authorized by a member. If the members do not want their names public, this is the place to use someone else to sign.

✪ The names of the *managers* or *managing members* can be listed, but the **ARTICLES** will be accepted without them. Some banks do not want to open accounts for companies if no manager or managing member is listed. If you leave it blank, you can always add the name when you file the company's annual report.

Paper Filing   If you prefer to mail in your **ARTICLES OF ORGANIZATION**, you can use the forms in the back of this book or you can download .pdf versions to print out at this website:

www.dos.state.fl.us/doc/form_download.html

The form is very straight-forward. You can use the guidance for online filing to fill out your hard copy form. The registered agent must sign on the first page and a member or anyone authorized by the member may sign the **ARTICLES OF ORGANIZATION**.

Professional LLCs   A professional limited liability company that is governed by Florida Statutes, Chapter 621, should include in its articles the limitations of that statute.

✪ The business purpose is limited to the practice of the one profession for which it was organized.

✪ No person or entity can be admitted as a member unless he, she, or it is qualified to practice the profession. Also, no interest can be sold except to someone so qualified.

This book contains **Articles of Organization** that can be used for professional LLCs. (see form 3, p.149.)

Submission of Articles

The **Articles of Organization** should be mailed to:

Registration Section
Division of Corporations
P.O. Box 6327
Tallahassee, FL 32314

You should send them along with a **Transmittal Letter** and the filing fees. (see form 1, p.143.) The fees are $125, which includes the **Articles of Organization** filing fee ($100) and the designation of registered agent fee ($25).

If you wish to receive a certified copy of the **Articles**, the cost is $30. This is usually an unnecessary expense because a certified copy is rarely, if ever, needed. The better alternative is to enclose a photocopy of the **Articles** and ask that it be "stamped with the filing date" and returned. For $5 you can get a certificate of status, but this, too, is not often needed.

The return time for the **Articles** is usually a week or two. If there is a need to have them back quickly, they may be sent by a courier, such as FedEx or Airborne Express, with prepaid return. In such cases, they are filed the day received and returned shortly thereafter. The address for courier delivery is:

Division of Corporations
Department of State
409 East Gaines Street
Tallahassee, FL 32399

CERTIFICATE OF CONVERSION

Entities such as partnerships, sole proprietorships, and business trusts may convert to limited liability companies by filing a **Certificate of Conversion** along with their **Articles of Organization**. (Fla. Stat. Sec. 608.439.) A blank form is included in this book for this purpose. The filing fee is $25. (see form 4, p.151.)

A corporation cannot convert to an LLC, but it may either sell its assets to an LLC and then dissolve or merge into an LLC. The provisions for merger with an LLC are contained in Florida Statutes, Sections 608.438 through 608.4384, which are included in Appendix A. Before changing a corporate business to an LLC, you should find out if there will be any negative tax consequences to the change.

CERTIFICATE OF MERGER AND PLAN OF MERGER

The **CERTIFICATE OF MERGER** and **PLAN OF MERGER** forms in this book are provided by the secretary of state. These only provide a basic outline of what is legally needed. The details must be filled in based on the current situation of your business. You should consult a tax professional to find out what type of merger would be most appropriate for your situation. (see form 5, p.153.)

OPERATING AGREEMENT OR MANAGEMENT AGREEMENT

As mentioned in the previous chapter, an LLC must decide if it will be managed by all the members or by a limited number of managers. If it is to be run by managers, there may be one or more, and he or she may or may not be a member.

It is important in either case to have a written agreement spelling out the rights and duties of the members and managers, if any. This is also a good document in which to include other rules governing the LLC. Even if an LLC has only one member, a membership agreement should be signed to formalize the LLC and make it clear that the member is not personally liable for the debts of the business.

The law of LLCs is very new, and since corporations that do not follow procedures can have their *veil pierced* (meaning the owners can be liable), it is possible that a court may do the same to an LLC. Therefore, it is important to set up procedures to formalize the company and distinguish it from its owners. Of course, if you set up procedures and do not follow them, a court could use that as a reason to impose liability.

Member-Managed Operating Agreement

In Appendix D, there is a generic **LIMITED LIABILITY COMPANY MEMBER-MANAGED OPERATING AGREEMENT**. (see form 10, p.169.) Use this form if your LLC will have one member or if it will have two or more members and be managed by all the members.

The generic **LIMITED LIABILITY COMPANY MEMBER-MANAGED OPERATING AGREEMENT** form has basic terms that can be useful to most businesses. If all of the terms apply to your business, you should execute a copy and keep it with your company records.

If there are other terms you would like to include in your agreement, you can add them in paragraph 21 or you can draw up an addendum to the membership agreement. Be sure to complete the **SCHEDULE A TO LIMITED LIABILITY COMPANY OPERATING OR MANAGEMENT AGREEMENT** and attach it to your agreement. (see form 12, p.177.)

Management Operating Agreement

In Appendix D there is a generic **MANAGEMENT OPERATING AGREEMENT**. (see form 11, p.173.) Use this form if your LLC will have two or more members and be managed by a limited number of members or by someone who is not a member.

The generic **MANAGEMENT OPERATING AGREEMENT** form has basic terms that can be useful to most businesses. If all of the terms apply to your business, you should execute a copy and keep it with your company records.

If there are other terms you would like to include in your agreement you can add them in paragraph 21 or you can draw up an addendum to the membership agreement. Be sure to complete the **SCHEDULE A TO OPERATING AGREEMENT** and attach it to your agreement. (see form 12, p.177.)

TAX FORMS

When starting your LLC, there is just one federal tax form all companies need to file. If you elect to be taxed as a corporation you will file

Taxpayer Identification Number

a second form, and if you are subject to Florida taxes you will need to register with the state.

The limited liability company must obtain a *taxpayer identification number*, also called an *employer identification number* (EIN)—the business equivalent of a Social Security number—prior to opening a bank account. This is done by filing **Application for Employer Identification Number** (IRS Form SS-4), included in this book. (see form 6, p.161.) This usually takes two or three weeks, so it should be filed early. Send the form to:

Internal Revenue Service Center
Atlanta, GA 39901-0102

If you would like to get the number quickly you can obtain it online in a matter of minutes. The online filing form is here:

https://sa.www4.irs.gov/sa_vign/newFormSS4.do

When you apply for this number, you will probably be put on the mailing list for other tax forms. If you do not receive these, you should call 800-829-3676 and request the forms for new businesses. These include Circular E that explains the taxes due, the W-4 forms for each employee, the tax deposit coupons, and IRS Form 941 quarterly return for withholding.

Entity Classification Election IRS Form 8832

IRS Form 8832 was issued by the IRS in 1997 to allow LLCs to choose their tax status. (see form 7, p.163.) It is basically a choice between partnership taxation and corporate taxation. For a single-member LLC, it is a choice between sole proprietorship taxation and corporate taxation.

The difference between the two types of taxation is that sole proprietorships and partnerships are not taxed at all, while corporations are treated like separate taxpayers. A sole proprietorship or partnership just reports its income and expenses; whereas the proprietor or partners report the net profit or loss on their personal tax returns. A corporation files a tax return and pays tax on any profits. If it distributes any of the profits to the members, those profits are taxed again. Therefore, it is better not to choose corporate taxation in most cases.

One way around the double taxation is if all of the profits can be paid to the members as salaries, thus making the profits deductible. The corporation then has no profit on which to pay tax. The problem arises when the company makes more money than would be reasonable to pay as salaries. The IRS can then impose extra corporate taxation on the excess amounts.

Another way around double taxation is for the LLC to opt for corporate taxation and then select S corporation status. To do so, you would file Form 8832 and Form 2553 within seventy-five days of forming your LLC.

State Taxes   If you prefer pass-through taxation, you do not need to file Form 8832 until the member files his or her tax return and then Form 8832 is included with that return.

If you will be collecting sales tax or will pay wages subject to unemployment tax, you will need to register with the state of Florida. To do this you will need to follow form DR-1. Also, if you opt to be taxed as a C corporation you will need to register to pay Florida's corporate income tax.

The forms needed can be obtained at on the Florida Department of Revenue's website at **www.myflorida.com/dor/forms** or you can call them at 800-352-3671 or 850-488-6800.

EMPLOYEES

An LLC that has employees other than its members is subject to numerous laws and reporting requirements, which are beyond the scope of this book. These include new hire reporting, federal wage withholding, state and federal unemployment compensation taxes, discrimination, minimum wage, and child labor posters.

BANK ACCOUNTS

A limited liability company must have a bank account. Checks payable to a limited liability company cannot be cashed—they must be deposited into an account. Unfortunately, many banks charge high rates to companies for the right to put their money in the bank. You can tell how much extra a company is being charged when you compare a corporate account to a personal account with similar activity. (For similar balance and activity, an individual might earn $6.00 interest for the month while a corporation pays $40.00 in bank fees.)

Fortunately, some banks have set up reasonable fees for small businesses, such as charging no fees if a balance of $1000 or $2500 is maintained. Because the fees can easily amount to hundreds of dollars a year, it pays to shop around. Even if the bank is relatively far from the business, using bank-by-mail can make the distance meaningless. However, do not be surprised if a bank with low fees raises them. Some companies may change banks as much as four times in one year as each bank raises its fees or is bought out by a bank with higher fees.

As the banking industry struggled for profits about a decade ago, most banks raised fees on business accounts. Even with their balance sheets improving, they are not eager to give up this new source of wealth. However, you can usually find loopholes if you use your imagination.

One trick is to open a checking account and a *money market account*. (Money market accounts pay higher interest and do not charge for making deposits. You can only write three checks a month but you can usually make unlimited withdrawals.) Make all of your deposits into the money market account and just pay bills out of the regular checking account, transferring funds as needed. However, banks are catching on to this and starting to charge for deposits into money market accounts. Nonetheless, you can start one at a brokerage firm.

Another way to save money in bank charges is to order checks from a private source rather than through the bank. These are usually much cheaper than those the bank offers because the bank makes a profit on the check printing. If the bank officer does not like the idea when you are opening the account, just wait until your first batch runs out and switch over without telling the bank. They probably will not even notice, as long as you get the checks printed correctly. While most *business* checks are large (and expensive), there is no reason you cannot use small *personal size* checks for your business. They are easier to carry around and work just as well.

Paperwork   All you should need to open a business bank account is a copy of your **ARTICLES OF ORGANIZATION** and your federal tax identification number. Some banks, however, want more.

If you have trouble opening the account, you can use the **BANKING RESOLUTION FORM** included with this book, or you can make up a similar form. (see form 15, p.183.)

LICENSES

Before opening your business, you might need a county occupational license, and if you will be working within a city, a city occupational license. Businesses that perform work in several cities, such as builders, must obtain a license from each city in which they work. This does not have to be done until you actually begin a job in a particular city.

Home Business   County occupational licenses can be obtained from the tax collector in the county courthouse. City licenses are usually available at city hall. Be sure to find out if *zoning* allows your type of business before buying or leasing property because the licensing departments will check the zoning before issuing your license.

Problems occasionally arise when a person attempts to start a business in his or her home. Small new businesses cannot afford to pay rent for commercial space and cities often try to forbid business in residential areas. Getting a county occupational license often gives notice to the city that a business is being conducted in a residential area.

Some people avoid the problem by starting their businesses without occupational licenses, figuring that the penalties are nowhere near the cost of office space. Others get the county license and ignore the city rules. If a person has commercial trucks and equipment parked on his or her property, there will probably be complaints by neighbors and the city will most likely take legal action. But if a person's business consists merely of making phone calls out of the home and keeping supplies inside the house, the problem may never surface.

If the problem does arise regarding a home business that does not disturb the neighbors, a good argument can be made that the zoning law that prohibits the business is unconstitutional. However, court battles with a city are expensive and probably not worth the effort for a small business. The best course of action is to keep a low profile. Using a post office box is sometimes helpful in diverting attention away from the residence. However, the secretary of state and the occupational license administrator will want a street address. There should be no problem using a residential address and explaining to the city that it is merely the corporate address and that no business is conducted on the premises.

chapter 6

Capital Structure and Selling Interests

Before setting up your LLC, you need to determine its financial structure as well as a plan for future expansion.

CAPITAL STRUCTURE

There is no hard and fast rule as to how much capital you should put into a limited liability company. The more you assign as capital, the more you have at risk in the business. Therefore, you want to deposit as little as possible. Keep in mind that if you contribute too little, a court might some day say you were undercapitalized and find you personally liable for company debts, just as it could for a corporation. Also, there could be tax problems with not counting enough of your contributions as capital or for contributing appreciated property. These matters should be discussed with a tax specialist.

If you are starting a small business that does not need a lot of expensive equipment, a thousand or a few thousand dollars would be a safe amount with which to start. If you do need to buy expensive equipment, and the company can borrow the money from a third party to cover it, you would probably be safe as well. However, if you need to purchase expensive equipment and personally loan the money to the company rather than contribute it as capital, you should weigh the risks of a lawsuit and consider consulting an attorney or accountant who specializes in business start-ups.

One thing to keep in mind is that if you do not put in the amount of capital you state in your initial agreement and are later sued or file bankruptcy, you may be required to come up with any unpaid amount because it may be considered an unpaid debt to the company. That is something you could be held personally liable for. In a grievous case a judge might use it as a reason to void the limited liability of the LLC.

PAYMENT FOR MEMBERSHIP INTERESTS

Florida law allows membership interests to be paid for with money, property, services, or a promissory note. The important thing to remember is that if a member fails to make the specified payment or takes the money back out (other than salary or profit), he or she may be liable to the company or its creditors for the full amount that should have been paid.

Some other things to consider include the following.

- If a member trades services for an interest in the capital of the company, he or she must pay income tax on the value of interest at the time the services are exchanged for the interest. (If the interest is only a share of future profits, the tax does not have to be paid until the profits are received.)

- When appreciated property is traded to an LLC in exchange for a membership interest, the tax basis of the property carries over to the membership interest. Taxes on the appreciation are paid when the member sells his or her LLC interest.

- If the LLC sells the property, it may have to pay a tax on the amount received over the contributor's basis.

Tax rules are complicated and ever-changing. If you will be doing creative financing, you should consult with a tax expert or a tax guide.

SECURITIES LAWS

The issuance of *securities* is subject to both federal and state securities laws. A *security* can include membership interests in the company and debts (notes, bonds, etc.). The laws covering securities are extremely broad. For example, in an enterprise in which the investor relies on the efforts of others for profit, any interest that represents an investment is considered a security. Even a promissory note for a loan has been held to be a security. Once an investment is determined to involve a security, strict rules apply. If the rules are not followed, there can be criminal penalties and civil damages can also be awarded to purchasers.

The rules are designed to protect people who put up money as an investment in a business. In the stock market crash of the 1930s, many people lost their life savings in swindles. The government wants to be sure that it will not happen again. Unfortunately, the laws can also make it difficult to raise capital for many honest businesses.

The goal of the laws covering sales of securities is that investors be given full disclosure of the risks involved in an investment. To accomplish this, the law usually requires that the securities must either be registered with the federal Securities and Exchange Commission, a similar state regulatory body, or that lengthy disclosure statements be compiled and distributed.

The law is complicated and strict compliance is required. The penalties are so harsh that most lawyers will not handle securities matters. Most likely, you would not be able to get through the registration process on your own. But, like your decision to start an LLC without a lawyer, you may wish to consider some alternatives when attempting to raise capital without a lawyer such as the following.

- ✪ Borrow the money as a personal loan from friends or relatives. The disadvantage is that you will have to pay them back personally if the business fails. However, you may have to do that anyway if they are close relatives or if you do not follow the securities laws.

- ✪ Tailor your stock issuance to fall within the exemptions in the securities laws. There are some exemptions in the securities laws for small businesses that may apply to your transaction. (See the next section.) The anti-fraud provisions always apply—even if the transaction is exempt from registration. Anti-fraud provisions forbid any misrepresentation of the financial condition of the business or concealment of negative financial aspects of the business.

You should make at least one appointment with a securities lawyer to be sure you have covered everything and that there have not been any changes in the law. You can often pay for an hour or so of a securities lawyer's time for $150 to $300 and just ask questions about your plans. He or she can tell you what not to do and what your options are. You can then make an informed decision.

For an explanation of Florida securities law, a good book is *Florida Small Business Practice,* published by the Florida Bar CLE division. It should be available in most law libraries. For technical laws and regulations of all fifty states, see the *Blue Sky Reporter,* also available at most law libraries.

Exemptions to Securities Laws

In most situations where one person, a husband and wife, or a few partners, run a business, and all parties are active in the enterprise, securities laws do not apply to their issuance of membership interests to themselves. These are the simple LLCs that are the subject of this book. As a practical matter, if a relative of yours wants to put up some money for an interest in your business, you probably will not get in trouble. They probably will not seek triple damages and criminal penalties if your business fails. However, this might not be true for you if someday your father-in-law becomes your ex-father-in-law.

If you wish to obtain money from additional investors, you might be able to do it in such a way as to be exempt from securities laws. The following sections explain exemptions to federal and Florida securities laws. By doing such things as avoiding advertising, limiting the number of investors, and only selling interests to wealthy individuals, you may fit into an exemption from securities laws. The following sections explain exemptions to federal and Florida securities laws.

FEDERAL EXEMPTIONS

The following are the federal exemptions to securities laws that are most useful to small businesses. Be sure to check the next section for exemptions to Florida securities laws.

Federal Private Placement Exemption

If you sell your stock to a small group of people without any advertising, you can fall into the *private offering exemption* if all of the following apply:

❂ all persons to whom offers are made are financially astute, are participants in the business, or have a substantial net worth;

❂ no advertising or general solicitation is used to promote the interests;

❂ the number of persons to whom the offers are made is limited;

❂ the shares are purchased for investment and not for immediate resale;

❂ the persons to whom the membership interest is offered are given all relevant information (including financial information) regarding the issuance and the LLC; and,

❂ a filing that claims the exemption is made upon the United States Securities and Exchange Commission.

Federal Intrastate Offering Exemption

If you only offer your securities to residents of one state, you may be exempt from federal securities laws. This is because federal laws usually only apply to interstate commerce. Intrastate offerings are covered by SEC Rule 147. If it is followed carefully, your sale will be exempt from federal registration.

Federal Small Offerings Exemptions

In recent years, the SEC has liberalized the rules in order to make it easier for business to grow. Under Regulation D, adopted by the Securities and Exchange Commission, there are three types of exemptions (under Rules 504, 505, and 506) that businesses can use when they are trying to raise money.

Under SEC Rule 504, offering of securities of up to $1,000,000 in a twelve-month period can be exempt. Under this rule, offers can be made to any number of persons, no specific information must be provided, and investors do not have to be sophisticated.

Under SEC Rule 505, an offering of up to $5,000,000 can be made in a twelve-month period, but no public advertising may be used and only thirty-five nonaccredited investors may purchase stock. Any number of accredited investors may purchase stock.

Accredited investors are sophisticated individuals with high net worth or high income, large trusts or investment companies, or persons involved in the business.

Under SEC Rule 506, there is no limit on the amount of money that may be raised, but like SEC Rule 505, it does not allow advertising and limits nonaccredited investors to thirty-five.

FLORIDA SECURITIES LAWS

Unfortunately, the simplification of federal requirements has not been accompanied by similar changes at the state level. Florida and most states still have much stricter requirements for the issuance of securities. There is a movement to change the laws, but for now, the only way to avoid the Florida registration procedures is to qualify for the Florida private placement.

Private Placement Exemption

The *private placement exemption* applies if all of the following are true:

❂   there are thirty-five or fewer purchasers of shares;

❂   no commissions are paid to anyone to promote the stock unless that person is a registered securities dealer;

❂   no advertising or general solicitation is used to promote the stock;

✪ all material information (including financial information) regarding the stock issuance and the company is given to or accessible to all shareholders; and,

✪ when sales are made to five or more persons, a three-day right of recision is given.

These rules may sound simple on the surface, but there are many more rules, regulations, and court cases explaining each one in more detail. For example, what does "thirty-five persons" mean? Sounds simple, but it can mean more than thirty-five persons. Spouses, persons whose net worth exceeds $1,000,000, and founders of the company may not be counted in some circumstances.

Each state has its own *blue sky* requirements and exemptions. If you are going to raise money from investors, check with a qualified securities lawyer.

Florida Division of Securities

As you can see, the exemption does not give you much latitude in raising money. Therefore, you will have to register for most issuances. For answers to specific questions on Florida securities registration, you can contact the Division of Securities of the Florida Office of Financial Regulation at 800-848-3792 or visit their website at **www.flofr.com/Licensing**.

Florida Division of Securities
Plaza Level
Tallahassee, FL 32399-0350
805-410-9805

INTERNET BUSINESS SALES

With the advent of the Internet, promoters of stock and other interests in businesses have a new way of reaching large numbers of people (most of whom are financially able to afford investments in securities). However, all securities laws apply to the Internet and they are being enforced. Recently, state attorney generals have issued *cease and desist orders* to promoters of business interests not registered in their states.

Under current law, you must be registered in a state in order to sell business interests to its residents. If you are not registered in a state, you must turn down any residents from that state that want to buy from you.

The Internet does have some sources of capital listed. The following sites may be helpful.

America's Business Funding Directory
www.businessfinance.com

U.S. Small Business Administration (SBA)
www.sba.gov

Inc. Magazine
http://mothra.inc.com/finance

NVST
www.nvst.com/pnvHome.asp

Running a Limited Liability Company

This chapter explains the procedure you need to follow in running your limited liability company.

DAY-TO-DAY ACTIVITIES

One benefit of the limited liability company is that it need not comply with the required formalities of a corporation. Since the entity is so new, it is not yet clear what, if any, requirements the courts may impose on a limited liability company. However, it is universally recognized that the requirements will be less strict than those for a corporation.

At this point, you should still have some rules for operation of the company such as a **LIMITED LIABILITY COMPANY MEMBER-MANAGED AGREEMENT** or a **LIMITED LIABILITY COMPANY MANAGEMENT OPERATING AGREEMENT** to be safe. (see form 10, p.169 or form 11, p.173.) Also, you should be sure to follow whatever rules that you have set for yourself.

One important point to remember is to keep the company separate from your personal affairs. Do not continuously make loans to yourself from company funds and do not commingle funds.

Minutes

The keeping of **MINUTES** is not specifically required of an LLC, but LLCs are so new that it is unclear what courts will require. Doing so may provide you with some additional protection from liability. To make this easy for you, a blank **MINUTES** form has been included in Appendix D. (see form 13, p.179.) A sample filled-in form is in Appendix C. Just make several copies of this form and fill one out whenever you make a major decision for the company.

Signing for Your LLC

Another important point to remember is that when you sign documents for the company, you must always use the full name of the company with the correct suffix (L.L.C., L.C., etc.) and always sign your name as a member of the company with your title. For example, you would sign:

Johnson & Smith, L.L.C., by John Johnson, member

If you do not, you may lose your protection from liability. There have been cases in which a person forgot to put his or her title after his or her name and was held personally liable for a company debt.

Certificate of Authority

An LLC is a relatively new entity; therefore, people dealing with one arc not always sure how to do so legally. Sometimes they ask for a form that contains the names of the persons who have the power to sign papers. The state of Florida does not have a special form for this purpose. If you sent a photocopy of your **ARTICLES OF ORGANIZATION** with the original, you should have gotten it back stamped by the secretary of state. This, along with the cover letter stating that you are registered, should be enough for most people. If they want more, you can use the **CERTIFICATE OF AUTHORITY** form included in Appendix D of this book. (see form 14, p.181.)

RECORDS

Florida Statutes Section 608.4101(1) requires that a limited liability company keep a set of records at its registered office, which includes the following information:

- ✪ a current list of the names and last known business, residence, or mailing addresses of all members and managers;

- a copy of the **ARTICLES OF ORGANIZATION** and all **CERTIFICATES OF CONVERSION**, and any powers of attorney used in executing them;

- copies of the company's income tax returns for the last three years;

- copies of any operating agreements currently in effect;

- copies of any financial statements for the company for the last three years; and,

- unless such information is contained in the **ARTICLES**, there must be a document setting out:

  - the amount of cash and the agreed upon value of any property or services contributed by each member or agreed to be contributed by each member;

  - the times or events at which any additional contributions must be made; and,

  - any events that would cause the company to dissolve and wind up its affairs.

These records must be available to members and their agents and attorneys. (Fla. Stat. Sec. 608.4101(2).) The records must be located at the LLC's principal office or other reasonable locations specified in the operating agreement. Records from the time they were members must also be made available to former members for proper purposes. The cost of labor and materials can be charged for the copies. Managers have the same right to examine the records as long as it concerns their duties.

The records of an LLC do not have to be kept in writing if they are kept in a form that can easily be converted to writing within a reasonable time. (Fla. Stat. Sec. 608.4101(5).) Although the statute is not specific, it is presumed to refer to an electronic format, rather than, say, a woven tapestry format.

REPORTS TO MEMBERS

Without being asked by the members, LLCs are required to provide its members (and representatives of deceased members) with any information the member reasonably needs to exercise his or her rights and duties under the operating agreement or the law. (Fla. Stat. Sec. 608.4101(3)(a).)

The company must provide, upon demand, other information requested unless such demand is unreasonable. (Fla. Stat. Sec. 608.4101(3)(b).)

MEMBER MEETINGS

There is no requirement for the members to meet regularly. But, once again, since the law is not settled in this area, the more formality you use, the greater protection you have against potential liability.

Meetings do not need to be held in person. They can be done over the phone or even by Internet chat. The important thing is to make some notes to keep a record of the meetings. This formality might protect you from liability.

It is a good idea to hold a meeting when major decisions are being made. If you are a one-member company, you can hold the meeting in your head. Just remember to fill out a **MINUTES** form with the company records. (see form 13, p.179.)

SALARIES

Some new businesses forgo salaries until they are profitable, but if you are able to start out in the black or borrow startup money, you could pay salaries from the beginning. You can generally set whatever salaries you want in a business with the following exceptions.

Too Low   You cannot set your salary unreasonably low to avoid Social Security and Medicare taxes. For example, if you paid yourself a $10,000 salary but took out $50,000 in profits, the IRS could argue that you underpaid Social Security and Medicare taxes.

Too High   Paying salaries that are too high could be a problem if it would defraud your creditors or investors. Check with your accountant as to what would be considered reasonable in your industry.

DISTRIBUTIONS

Typically, an LLC will pay salaries to some or all members. Also, when profits allow, the LLC can distribute a lump sum among its members. How distributions are made is usually set out in the operating agreement. If the operating agreement is silent as to distributions, the company should follow Florida Statutes Section 608.426. You should also check with your tax advisor as to the best way to take out profits in your situation.

An LLC is not allowed to make a distribution if such distribution would render the company *insolvent*. Managers and members who assent to, or accept, a distribution that makes the company insolvent can be held personally liable. (Fla. Stat. Secs. 608.426(3) and 608.428.)

This means that if you take money out of the company making it unable to meet its normal obligations, you may be forced to pay that money back. For example, if the company has several debts and you sell off its main asset and take proceeds out yourself, the creditors may be able to sue you personally for that money. But there are a lot of fine points and exceptions to this rule, so if you get into such a situation you should check with an accountant or attorney to get advice as to what would be permissible.

LOANS

If you loan money to your LLC or borrow money from it, you should always document both the loan and the repayment. One of the biggest mistakes people make in running a small business is to treat it like another checking account. This can cause you to lose your liability protection.

Generally you should make loans in round rather large amounts like $1000 or $5000. Do not use your company check to pay your bills and then pay it back at the end of the month.

You should use a promissory note and sign and date it. When you pay it off, write "paid" on it and keep it with your records. The better records you have, the better it will be for you if someone challenges you on formality.

TAXES

As explained earlier, an LLC can decide if it wants to be taxed as a corporation or to pass its income through to the members. If it elected to be taxed as a corporation then it would file either Form 1120 (C corporation taxation) or Form 1120-S (S corporation taxation).

If it elects to be a pass-through entity, it will file Form 1065 if there is more than one member. If there is just one member, he or she would report the income on his or her personal return (usually Schedule C if earned income, or Schedule E if rental income).

If a single-member LLC is owned by another LLC or by a corporation, the income would still be passed through to the owner's return, and no separate return would need to be filed for the single-member LLC. Normal monthly or quarterly returns would still need to be filed to report federal employment taxes, state sales taxes, and other periodic filings, just as for any other business.

ANNUAL REPORT

Each year the LLC must file an annual report between January 1 and April 30. The secretary of state sends out a postcard to each LLC informing it that it can file online or it can return the postcard for a paper form to file. The filing fee for the annual report is $50. If the report is not filed the LLC will be dissolved. To reinstate the company the fee is $150.

chapter 8

Amending a Limited Liability Company

Sometimes you may need to make changes to the structure of your limited liability company. This chapter explains how to make them legally.

ARTICLES OF ORGANIZATION

The **ARTICLES OF ORGANIZATION** are simple and therefore rarely need to be amended. If you need to do so, however, you can either file a correction or an amendment.

Correcting Articles

If the **ARTICLES** filed with the Department of State contain a false or erroneous statement, or were defectively signed, they can be corrected within thirty business days of filing by filing **ARTICLES OF CORRECTION**. (see form 16, p.185.) It should be filed with the Secretary of State with a filing fee of $25.

Amending Articles

The **ARTICLES OF ORGANIZATION** may be amended by filing **ARTICLES OF AMENDMENT** with the secretary of state. (see form 17, p.187.) This document must contain the following information:

- ✪ the name of the limited liability company;

✪   the date of filing of the original **Articles of Organization**; and,

✪   the amendments being made to the articles.

Restated Articles

A limited liability company may file restated **Articles of Organization** at any time it wishes to consolidate articles contained in various amendments. The restated articles may merely include prior changes or may include new changes. If they merely restate changes, they must be titled *restated articles of organization*; and if they add changes, they must be titled *amended and restated articles of organization*. The titles may include any other wording the company deems appropriate.

Prepare the restated articles by including:

✪   the company's current name;

✪   the original name, if any;

✪   the date of filing of the original articles;

✪   the effective date of the restated articles if not effective upon filing;

✪   a statement that they were duly executed and filed in accordance with Fla. Stat. Sec. 608.411; and,

✪   if the restated articles merely restate the existing articles, do not amend them, and there is no discrepancy.

OPERATING AGREEMENT OR MANAGEMENT AGREEMENT

Your operating agreement or **Management Agreement** should contain a section spelling out the procedure for amending the agreement. When you decide to amend the agreement, you should be sure to follow the procedures required and to document the vote in your **Minutes**.

REGISTERED AGENT
OR REGISTERED OFFICE

To change the registered agent or registered office, a **STATEMENT OF CHANGE OF REGISTERED OFFICE OR REGISTERED AGENT OR BOTH** must be sent to the secretary of state with the fee of $25. (see form 18, p.189.) This form can be used to change both the registered agent and the registered office, or to just change one of them. If you are changing just one, such as the agent, list the registered office as both the old address and the new address.

MERGING WITH ANOTHER BUSINESS

Florida statutes provide numerous rules covering mergers of LLCs. (Fla. Stat. Secs. 608.438 through 608.4384.) These are included in Appendix A of this book. The secretary of state supplies both **CERTIFICATE OF MERGER** and a **PLAN OF MERGER**. (see form 5, p.153.)

However, if not done properly, a merger can have negative tax consequences for an existing business. Before completing these forms, you should check with a tax professional who can suggest the best way to structure your merger.

RESIGNATIONS

Sometimes a person involved with an LLC wants to resign and have his or her name removed from the records of the company. For a member, managing member, or manager, this can be done by filing a **RESIGNATION OF MEMBER, MANAGING MEMBER, OR MANAGER** with the secretary of state and paying $25. (see form 20, p.193.)

For a registered agent to resign the form is **RESIGNATION OF REGISTERED AGENT** and the fee is $85 if the company is active and $25 if the company is dissolved. (see form 19, p.191.)

Dissolving a Limited Liability Company

This chapter explains how to dissolve and wind down the affairs of a limited liability company. Since this is a book about forming your limited liability company, not dissolving it, the circumstances regarding dissolution are not gone into great detail. However, the various types of dissolutions and certain matters surrounding are discussed.

ADMINISTRATIVE DISSOLUTION

If your limited liability company has ceased to do business and you no longer need to keep it active, it is not necessary to take any special action to dissolve it because it will be automatically dissolved if you fail to file your annual report. An LLC that has been administratively dissolved is still allowed to continue its existence to the extent necessary to wind up its affairs.

If your company has some debts that it is unable to pay at the time of dissolution, you would be better off formally dissolving it or having it file for bankruptcy. Otherwise, there is a chance you could be held personally liable for the debts.

If you think you might need to reinstate the company at some time in the future, it would be better to dissolve it formally. If it is dissolved for not filing, there are penalties of hundreds of dollars. It is cheaper to start a new LLC than to reinstate one that has been dissolved administratively.

EVENTS REQUIRING DISSOLUTION

Florida Statutes Section 608.441 require that an LLC file **ARTICLES OF DISSOLUTION** upon occurrence of any of the following:

- ✪ if the term of the LLC expires (if the term is for a set number of years and not perpetual);

- ✪ in the occurrence of any other event that requires dissolution under the **ARTICLES OF ORGANIZATION** or operating agreement;

- ✪ if a circuit court orders dissolution;

- ✪ if the members unanimously agree in writing to dissolve; or,

- ✪ if the LLC no longer has members. However, unless prohibited by company documents, the company has ninety days to admit a member. (Fla. Stat. Sec. 608.441(1)(d).)

If any of the above events happen, the LLC is required to file **ARTICLES OF DISSOLUTION** with the secretary of state and pay the $25 filing fee. (see form 21, p.195.)

NOTE: *Unless otherwise provided in the* **ARTICLES**, *the death, retirement, resignation, expulsion, bankruptcy, or dissolution of a member does not cause the dissolution of the LLC.*

ARTICLES OF DISSOLUTION

An advantage of formal dissolution is that having given proper notice to creditors and a period of time has passed, there is no risk that they can come back against the members. To formally dissolve a limited liability company, **ARTICLES OF DISSOLUTION** must be filed with the secretary of state. The form for dissolution of an LLC is included in this book. (see form 21, p.195.) (Fla. Stat. Sec. 608.445.) The form is straightforward and can be completed with no problem.

Under Florida Statutes Section 608.4431, an LLC may not carry on business after dissolution, but it can continue its existence for the purpose of:

- ✪ collecting its assets;

- ✪ disposing of property that will not be distributed to members;

- ✪ discharging liabilities;

- ✪ distributing assets to creditors and members; and,

- ✪ doing anything else necessary to wind up its affair.

REVOCATION OF DISSOLUTION

An LLC may *undissolve* within 120 days of filing **ARTICLES OF DISSOLUTION** by filing **ARTICLES OF REVOCATION OF DISSOLUTION** with the secretary of state along with the $100 filing fee. (see form 22, p.199.) (Fla. Stat., Sec. 608.4411.)

JUDICIAL DISSOLUTION

A court may dissolve an LLC under certain circumstances if so requested by:

- ✪ the Florida Department of Legal Affairs;

- ✪ a manager or member;

- ✪ a creditor; or,

- ✪ the LLC.

For details on the procedures for judicial dissolution, see Florida Statutes, Sections 608.449 through 608.4493, contained in Appendix A.

DISTRIBUTION OF ASSETS

When an LLC dissolves, the assets of the company must be distributed in the following order:

✪   to creditors, including members who are creditors;

✪   to members and former members in satisfaction of liabilities under Florida Statutes Sections 608.426 and 608.427; and,

✪   to members in proportion to their capital accounts.

For more information, see Florida Statutes Section 608.444 in Appendix A.

BANKRUPTCY

If your company is in debt beyond its means, it can file for bankruptcy. *Chapter 7 bankruptcy* is for liquidation and *Chapter 11 bankruptcy* is for reorganization of debts. If the debts are small and there is little chance the creditors will pursue collection, bankruptcy is unnecessary. You can allow the state to dissolve the company for failure to file the annual report. However, if the debts are large and you fear the creditors will attempt to collect the debt from the officers or directors, you should go through formal bankruptcy and/or dissolution. Such a scenario is beyond the scope of this book. You should consult an attorney or bankruptcy text for further guidance.

Glossary

A

annual report. Annual report that each Florida LLC must file with the secretary of state.

articles of organization. The legal document used to form a limited liability company that sets out basic information about it, such as its name.

assignment. The transfer of legal rights to another person or entity.

B

blue sky laws. Laws governing the sales of securities.

C

C corporation. A corporation that pays taxes on its profits.

charging order. A court order directed at an interest in an LLC.

corporation. An artificial legal person that is set up to conduct a business owned by shareholders and run by officers and directors.

D

distributions. Money paid out to owners of a corporation or limited liability company.

E

employee. Person who works for another under that person's control and direction.

employer identification number. Number issued by the Internal Revenue Service to identify taxpayers who do not have Social Security numbers.

F

fictitious name. A name used by a business that is not its personal or legal name.

G

general partnership. A business that is owned by two or more persons.

I

independent contractor. A person who does work as a separate business rather than as an employee.

insolvent. Being without enough assets or income to pay debts.

intangible tax. The Florida tax on intangible personal property.

L

liability. The legal responsibility to pay for an injury.

limited liability company. An artificial legal person set up to conduct a business owned and run by members.

limited liability partnership. An artificial legal person set up to conduct a business owned and run by members, which is set up for professionals such as attorneys or doctors.

limited partnership. A business that is owned by two or more persons of which one or more is liable for the debts of the business and one or more has no liability for the debts.

M

management agreement. The document that controls the operation of a limited liability company that is managed by managers.

manager. A person who controls the operations of a limited liability company.

manager-managed LLC. A limited liability company that is controlled by one or more managers who are not all of the members of the company.

member. Person owning an interest in a limited liability company.

member-managed LLC. A limited liability company that is controlled by all of its members.

minority interest owners. The owners of an interest in an LLC who own less than a majority interest.

minutes. Records of the proceedings of business meetings.

O

occupational license. A government-issued permit to transact business.

operating agreement. A contract among members of a limited liability company spelling out how the company is to be run.

organizational meeting. The meeting of the founders of a corporation or limited liability company in which the company is structured and ready to begin business.

P

partnership. A business formed by two or more persons.

piercing the corporate veil. When a court ignores the corporate structure to hold the owners of the business liable.

promoters. Persons who start a business venture and usually offer interests for sale to investors.

proprietorship. A business that is owned by one person.

R

registered agent. A person who is designated by a limited liability company to receive legal papers for the company.

registered office. A physical location where the registered agent of a limited liability company can receive legal papers for the company.

regulations. The former name of the operating agreement of a limited liability company.

S

S corporation. A corporation in which the profits are taxed to the shareholders.

securities. Interests in a business such as stock or bonds.

series limited liability company. A company that can segregate assets into separate sub-entities so that liability can be limited to single assets.

T

trademark. A name or symbol used to identify the source of goods or services.

U

unemployment compensation. Payments to a former employee who was terminated from a job for a reason not based on his or her fault.

Z

zoning. Laws that regulate the use of real estate.

For Further Reference

As mentioned earlier in this book, the LLC laws are new and still developing. To keep up-date-on changes in the law, the following sites are good places to do legal research:

www.lawschool.cornell.edu/lawlibrary

www.findlaw.com

The following books provide in-depth analysis of LLC law. Some are expensive, but may be found in larger law libraries.

Callison, J. William, and Maureen A. Sullivan. *Limited Liability Companies: A State-by-State Guide to Law and Practice*. Eagan: West Group.

Cunningham, John M. *Drafting Limited Liability Company Operating Agreements*. New York: Aspen Publishers.

Rubenstein, Jeffrey C., et al. *Limited Liability Companies: Law, Practice and Forms*. Seattle: Shepards.

Tuthill, Walter C. *Limited Liability Companies: Legal Aspects of Organization, Operation, and Dissolution*. Washington, D.C.: BNA.

Appendix A:
Florida LLC Statues
and Name Rules

Included in this appendix are the Florida Statutes covering limited liability companies. If you have questions that are beyond the scope of this book, these statutes may answer them. (Since the statutes are relatively new, there are not many court cases interpreting them.)

This appendix includes the following:

Florida Statutes Chapter 608 - Florida Limited Liability Company Act

Florida Statutes Chapter 621 - Professional Service Corporation and Limited Liability Company Act

To check future changes in the law, you can find Florida statutes at:

www.leg.state.fl.us

CHAPTER 608
LIMITED LIABILITY COMPANIES

608.401 Short title.—
Sections 608.401-608.705 may be cited as the "Florida Limited Liability Company Act."
History.—
s. 2, ch. 82-177; s. 4, ch. 93-284; s. 1, ch. 99-315; s. 1, ch. 2002-272.

608.402 Definitions.—
As used in this chapter:

(1) "Articles of merger" means initial, amended, and restated articles of merger of a limited liability company delivered to the Department of State in accordance with s. 608.4382. In the case of a foreign limited liability company, the term includes all records serving a similar function required to be filed with the Department of State or other official having custody of the records of the foreign limited liability company in the state or country under whose law it is organized.

(2) "Articles of organization" means initial, amended, and restated articles of organization of a limited liability company, including initial, amended, or restated articles of merger, if any. In the case of a foreign limited liability company, the term includes all records serving a similar function required to be filed with the Department of State or other official having custody of the records of the foreign limited liability company in the state or country under whose law it is organized.

(3) "Authorized representative" means one or more persons acting to form a limited liability company by executing and filing the articles of organization of such limited liability company in accordance with this chapter and authorized by a member of such limited liability company, which authorized representative may, but need not be, a member of the limited liability company that the authorized representative forms.

(4) "Bankruptcy" means an event that causes a person to cease to be a member as provided in s. 608.4237.

(5) "Business" means every trade, occupation, or profession and other lawful business, purpose, or activity, whether or not carried on for profit.

(6) "Capital account" means the agreed value of the initial contributions as provided in s. 608.4211, increased by the agreed value of subsequent contributions to capital, if any, and reduced by distributions of capital, unless otherwise provided in the articles of organization or the operating agreement.

(7) "Contribution" means any cash, property, or services rendered or a promissory note or other obligation to contribute cash or property or to perform services, which a person contributes to the limited liability company as a member.

(8) "Conveyance" means any assignment, transfer, sale, lease, mortgage, hypothecation, or encumbrance.

(9) "Court" includes every court and judge having jurisdiction in the action.

(10) "Distribution" means a direct or indirect transfer of money or other property or incurrence of indebtedness by a limited liability company to or for the benefit of its members in respect of their economic interests.

(11) "Entity" means, without limitation, any corporation; unincorporated association or business; limited liability company; business trust, real estate investment trust, common law trust, or other trust, general partnership, limited liability partnership, limited partnership, limited liability limited partnership, joint venture, or two or more persons having a joint or common economic interest; any state, local, federal, or foreign government, governmental subdivision, agency, or instrumentality; or any other domestic or foreign entity that is formed pursuant to the provisions of applicable law.

(12) "Foreign limited liability company" means a limited liability company formed under the laws of any state other than Florida or under the laws of any foreign country or other foreign jurisdiction.

(13) "Individual" means a natural person and includes the estate of a natural person.

(14) "Insolvent" means the inability of a limited liability company to pay the limited liability company's debts as they become due in the ordinary course of business or that the fair value of the limited liability company's total assets would be less than the sum of its total liabilities plus the amount that would be needed, if the limited liability company were to be dissolved and terminated at the time of the distribution, to satisfy the preferential distribution rights of the limited liability company's members accrued through such dissolution and termination.

(15) "Knowledge" means a person's actual knowledge of a fact, and does not include constructive knowledge of a fact.

(16) "Limited liability company" or "company" means a limited liability company organized and existing under this chapter.

(17) "Majority-in-interest of the members" means, unless otherwise provided in the articles of organization or operating agreement, members owning more than 50 percent of the then-current percentage or other interest in the profits of the limited liability company.

(18) "Manager" means a person who is appointed or elected to manage a manager-managed company and, unless otherwise provided in the articles of organization or operating agreement, a manager may be, but need not be, a member of the limited liability company.

(19) "Manager-managed company" means a limited liability company that is designated to be managed by one or more managers.

(20) "Managing member" means a member appointed or elected as a managing member of a member-managed company.

(21) "Member" means any person who has been admitted to a limited liability company as a member in accordance with this chapter and has an economic interest in a limited liability company which may, but need not, be represented by a capital account or, in the case of a foreign limited liability company, has been admitted to a limited liability company as a member in accordance with the laws of the state or foreign country or other foreign jurisdiction under which the foreign limited liability company is organized.

(22) "Member-managed company" means a limited liability company other than a manager-managed company.

(23) "Membership interest," "member's interest," or "interest" means a member's share of the profits and the losses of the limited liability company, the right to receive distributions of the limited liability company's assets, voting rights, management rights, or any other rights under this chapter or the articles of organization or operating agreement.

(24) "Operating agreement" means, subject to s. 608.423, written or oral provisions that are adopted for the management and regulation of the affairs of the limited liability company and that set forth the relationships of the members, managers, or managing members and the limited liability company. The term includes amendments to the operating agreement.

(25) "Person" means an individual or an entity.

(26) "Personal or other legal representative" means, as to a natural person, the executor, administrator, guardian, conservator, or other legal representative of the natural person and, as to a person other than a natural person, the legal representative or successor of such person.
History.—
s. 2, ch. 82-177; s. 53, ch. 83-216; s. 5, ch. 93-284; s. 1, ch. 99-315; s. 2, ch. 2002-272.

608.403 Purpose.—
A limited liability company may be organized under this chapter for any lawful purpose, but remains subject to statutes and regulations of the laws of this state for regulating and controlling its business, which shall control when in conflict with this chapter.
History.—
s. 2, ch. 82-177; s. 1, ch. 99-315.
608.404 Powers.—
Unless its articles of organization or operating agreement provide otherwise, each limited liability company organized and existing under this chapter shall have the same powers as an individual to do all things necessary to carry out its business and affairs, including, without limitation, the power to:
(1) Sue and be sued, and defend, in its name.
(2) Purchase, receive, lease, or otherwise acquire, own, hold, improve, use, and otherwise deal with real or personal property, or any legal or equitable interest in property, wherever located.
(3) Sell, convey, mortgage, grant a security interest in, lease, exchange, and otherwise encumber or dispose of all or any part of its property.
(4) Purchase, receive, subscribe for, or otherwise acquire, own, hold, vote, use, sell, mortgage, lend, grant a security interest in, or otherwise dispose of and deal in and with, shares or other interests in or obligations of any other entity.
(5) Make contracts or guarantees, or incur liabilities; borrow money; issue its notes, bonds, or other obligations, which may be convertible into or include the option to purchase other securities of the limited liability company; or make contracts of guaranty and suretyship which are necessary or convenient to the conduct, promotion, or attainment of the business of a corporation the majority of the outstanding stock of which is owned, directly or indirectly, by the contracting limited liability company; a corporation which owns, directly or indirectly, a majority of the outstanding membership interests of the contracting limited liability company; or a corporation the majority of the outstanding stock of which is owned, directly or indirectly, by a corporation which owns, directly or indirectly, the majority of the outstanding membership interests of the contracting limited liability company, which contracts of guaranty and suretyship shall be deemed to be necessary or convenient to the conduct, promotion, or attainment of the business of the contracting limited liability company; or make other contracts of guaranty and suretyship which are necessary or convenient to the conduct, promotion, or attainment of the business of the contracting limited liability company.
(6) Lend money, invest or reinvest its funds, and receive and hold real or personal property as security for repayment.
(7) Conduct its business, locate offices, and exercise the powers granted by this chapter within or without this state.
(8) Select managers or managing members and appoint officers, directors, employees, and agents of the limited liability company, define their duties, fix their compensation, and lend them money and credit.
(9) Make donations for the public welfare or for charitable, scientific, or educational purposes.
(10) Pay pensions and establish pension plans, pension trusts, profit-sharing plans, bonus plans, option plans, and benefit or incentive plans for any or all of its current or former managers, members, officers, agents, and employees.
(11) Be a promoter, incorporator, shareholder, partner, member, associate, or manager of any corporation, partnership, joint venture, trust, or other entity.
(12) Make payments or donations or do any other act not inconsistent with law that furthers the business of the limited liability company.

History.—
s. 2, ch. 82-177; s. 54, ch. 83-216; s. 6, ch. 93-284; s. 47, ch. 97-102; s. 1, ch. 99-315; s. 3, ch. 2002-272.
608.405 Formation.—
One or more persons may form a limited liability company.
History.—
s. 2, ch. 82-177; s. 7, ch. 93-284; s. 12, ch. 98-101.
608.406 Limited liability company name.—
(1) A limited liability company name:
(a) Must contain the words "limited liability company," the abbreviation "L.L.C.," or the designation "LLC" as the last words of the name of every limited liability company formed under the provisions of this chapter. The word "limited" may be abbreviated as "Ltd.," and the word "company" may be abbreviated as "Co." Omission of the words "limited liability company," the abbreviation "L.L.C.," or the designation "LLC" in the use of the name of the limited liability company shall render any person who knowingly participates in the omission, or knowingly acquiesces in the omission, liable for any indebtedness, damage, or liability caused by the omission.
(b) May not contain language stating or implying that the limited liability company is organized for a purpose other than that permitted in this chapter and its articles of organization.
(c) May not contain language stating or implying that the limited liability company is connected with a state or federal government agency or a corporation or other entity chartered under the laws of the United States.
(2) The name of the limited liability company must be distinguishable on the records of the Division of Corporations of the Department of State, except for fictitious name registrations filed pursuant to s. 865.09 and general partnership registrations filed pursuant to s. 620.8105; however, a limited liability company may register under a name that is not otherwise distinguishable on the records of the Division of Corporations with written consent of the owner entity provided the consent is filed with the Division of Corporations at the time of registration of such name.
(3) The name of the limited liability company shall be filed with the Department of State for public notice only and shall not alone create any presumption of ownership beyond that which is created under the common law.
(4) In the case of any limited liability company in existence prior to July 1, 2007, and registered with the Division of Corporations, the requirement in this section that the name of the entity be distinguishable from the names of other entities and filings shall not apply except when the limited liability company files documents on or after July 1, 2007, that would otherwise have affected its name.
History.—
s. 2, ch. 82-177; s. 8, ch. 93-284; s. 11, ch. 98-101; s. 1, ch. 99-315.
608.407 Articles of organization.—
(1) In order to form a limited liability company, articles of organization of a limited liability company shall be filed with the Department of State by one or more members or authorized representatives of the limited liability company. The articles of organization shall set forth:
(a) The name of the limited liability company, which must satisfy the requirements of s. 608.406.
(b) The mailing address and the street address of the principal office of the limited liability company.
(c) The name and street address of its initial registered agent for service of process in the state. The articles of organization shall include or be accompanied by the written statement required by s. 608.415.
(d) Any other matters that the members elect to include in the articles of organization.

(2) A limited liability company is formed at the time described in s. 608.409 if the person filing the articles of organization has substantially complied with the requirements of this section.

(3) The articles of organization shall be executed by at least one member or the authorized representative of a member.

(4) If the limited liability company is to be managed by one or more managers, the articles of organization may, but need not, include a statement that the limited liability company is to be a manager-managed company.

(5) The fact that articles of organization are on file with the Department of State is notice that the entity formed in connection with the filing of the articles of organization is a limited liability company formed under the laws of this state. If the articles of organization contain any information described in subsections (4) and (6), the articles of organization shall be deemed notice of that information as well, provided, if such information has been added or changed by an amendment or restatement of the articles of organization, the articles of organization shall not be deemed notice of such fact until 90 days after the effective date of such amendment or restatement.

(6) The articles of organization may also, but need not, identify one or more persons authorized to serve as a manager or managing member and may describe any limitations upon the authority of a manager or managing member, provided a provision in the articles of organization limiting the authority of a manager or managing member to transfer real property held in the name of the limited liability company is not notice of the limitation, to a person who is not a member or manager of the limited liability company, unless the limitation appears in an affidavit, certificate, or other instrument that bears the name of the limited liability company and is recorded in the office for recording transfers of such real property.

History.—
s. 2, ch. 82-177; s. 55, ch. 83-216; s. 11, ch. 93-284; s. 48, ch. 97-102; ss. 3, 13, ch. 98-101; s. 1, ch. 99-315; s. 4, ch. 2002-272; s. 4, ch. 2005-267.

608.408 Execution of articles, certificate, or statement.—
(1) Any articles, certificate, or statement required by this chapter to be filed with the Department of State must be executed in the following manner:

(a) If it is the articles of organization, a certificate of conversion, or a statement of change of registered agent or registered office, it must be signed by a member or by the authorized representative of a member, and by the new registered agent, if applicable; and

(b) If it is the articles of dissolution or revocation of dissolution, it must be signed by members having the same percentage of membership interests necessary to approve the dissolution or revocation of dissolution.

(2) Any person may sign a certificate through an attorney in fact, but a power of attorney to sign a certificate or statement authorizing the admission of a member must specifically describe the admission.

(3) The execution of a certificate constitutes an affirmation by the person executing the certificate, under the penalties of perjury, that the facts stated therein are true.

(4) If the articles of organization contain or any other document authorized or required to be filed under this chapter contains a false statement, one who suffers loss by reliance on the statement may recover damages for the loss from a person who signed the record or caused another to sign it on the person's behalf and knew the statement to be false at the time the record was signed.

History.—
s. 2, ch. 82-177; s. 56, ch. 83-216; s. 12, ch. 93-284; s. 1, ch. 99-315; s. 5, ch. 2002-272.

608.4081 Filing requirements.—
(1) To be filed by the Department of State, a document must satisfy the following requirements, as supplemented or modified by any other section of this chapter:

(a) This chapter must require or permit filing the document by the Department of State.

(b) The document must be executed as required by s. 608.408.

(c) The document must contain any information required by this chapter and may contain other information the limited liability company elects to include.

(d) The document must be typewritten or printed and must be legible.

(e) The document must be in the English language. A limited liability company name need not be in English if written in English letters or Arabic or Roman numerals, and the certificate of existence required of a foreign limited liability company need not be in English if accompanied by a reasonably authenticated English translation.

(f) If the Department of State has prescribed a mandatory form for the document, the document must be in or on the prescribed form.

(g) The document must be delivered to the Department of State for filing and must be accompanied by the correct filing fee and any other tax or penalty required by this chapter or other law.

(2) The document may be accompanied by one exact or conformed copy.

(3) Any signature on any certificate authorized to be filed by the Department of State under any provision of this chapter may be a facsimile, a conformed signature, or an electronically transmitted signature.

History.—
s. 13, ch. 93-284; s. 1, ch. 99-315; s. 6, ch. 2002-272.

608.4082 Filing duties of Department of State.—
(1) The Department of State files a document by stamping or otherwise endorsing the document as "filed," together with the Secretary of State's official title and the date and time of receipt. After filing a document, the Department of State shall deliver an acknowledgment or certified copy of the document to the domestic or foreign limited liability company or its representative.

(2) The Department of State shall return any document the department refuses to file to the domestic or foreign limited liability company or its representative within 15 days after the document was received for filing, together with a brief, written explanation of the reason for refusal.

(3) If the applicant returns the document with corrections in accordance with the rules of the Department of State within 60 days after it was mailed to the applicant by the Department of State and if at the time of return the applicant so requests in writing, the filing date of the document shall be the filing date that would have been applied had the original document not been deficient, except as to persons who justifiably relied on the record before correction and were adversely affected thereby.

(4) The Department of State's duty to file documents under this section is ministerial. Filing or refusing to file a document does not:

(a) Affect the validity or invalidity of the document in whole or part;

(b) Relate to the correctness or incorrectness of information contained in the document;

(c) Create a presumption that the document is valid or invalid or that information contained in the document is correct or incorrect.

(5) If not otherwise provided by law and the provisions of this chapter, the Department of State shall determine, by rule, the appropriate format for, number of copies of, manner of

execution of, method of electronic transmission of, and amount of and method of payment of fees for, any document placed under its jurisdiction.

History.—

s. 14, ch. 93-284; s. 1, ch. 99-315.

608.409 Effect of filing and issuance of time and date endorsement on the articles of organization.—

(1) Unless a delayed effective date is specified, the limited liability company's existence begins at the date and time when the articles of organization are filed, as evidenced by the Department of State's date and time endorsement on the original document, or on a date specified in the articles of organization, if such date is within 5 business days prior to the date of filing.

(2) The articles of organization may specify a delayed effective time and date of commencement of the limited liability company's existence, and if so specified, the articles of organization shall become effective, and the limited liability company's existence shall commence, at the time and date specified. If a delayed effective date, but no time, is specified, the articles of organization shall become effective, and the limited liability company's existence shall commence, at the close of business on the delayed effective date. Unless otherwise permitted by this chapter, a delayed effective date for a document may not be later than the 90th day after the date on which the document is filed.

(3) The Department of State's filing of the articles of organization is conclusive proof that all conditions precedent to organization have been satisfied except in a proceeding by the state to cancel or revoke the organization or to administratively dissolve the organization.

(4) A limited liability company shall not transact business or incur indebtedness, except that which is incidental to its organization or to obtaining subscriptions for or payment of contributions, until the effective date and time of the commencement of the limited liability company's existence.

History.—

s. 2, ch. 82-177; s. 57, ch. 83-216; s. 15, ch. 93-284; s. 1, ch. 99-315; s. 7, ch. 2002-272.

608.4101 Records to be kept; right to information.—

(1) Each limited liability company shall keep at its principal office the following records:

(a) A current list of the full names and last known business, residence, or mailing addresses of all members, managers, and managing members.

(b) A copy of the articles of organization, all certificates of conversion, and any other documents filed with the Department of State concerning the limited liability company, together with executed copies of any powers of attorney pursuant to which any articles of organization or certificates were executed.

(c) Copies of the limited liability company's federal, state, and local income tax returns and reports, if any, for the 3 most recent years.

(d) Copies of any then-effective operating agreement and any financial statements of the limited liability company for the 3 most recent years.

(e) Unless contained in the articles of organization or the operating agreement, a writing setting out:

1. The amount of cash and a description and statement of the agreed value of any other property or services contributed by each member and which each member has agreed to contribute.

2. The times at which or events on the happening of which any additional contributions agreed to be made by each member are to be made.

3. Any events upon the happening of which the limited liability company is to be dissolved and its affairs wound up.

(2) A limited liability company shall provide members and their agents and attorneys access to its records at the limited liability company's principal office or other reasonable locations specified in the operating agreement. The limited liability company shall provide former members and their agents and attorneys access for proper purposes to records pertaining to the period during which they were members. The right of access provides the opportunity to inspect and copy records during ordinary business hours. The limited liability company may impose a reasonable charge, limited to the costs of labor and material, for copies of records furnished.

(3) A limited liability company shall furnish to a member, and to the legal representative of a deceased member or member under legal disability:

(a) Without demand, information concerning the limited liability company's business or affairs reasonably required for the proper exercise of the member's rights and performance of the member's duties under the operating agreement or this chapter; and

(b) On demand, other information concerning the limited liability company's business or affairs, except to the extent the demand or the information demanded is unreasonable or otherwise improper under the circumstances.

(4) Each manager shall have the right to examine all of the information described in subsection (1) for a purpose reasonably related to his or her position as a manager. The manager of a limited liability company shall have the right to keep confidential from the members, for such period of time as the manager deems reasonable, any information which the manager reasonably believes to be in the nature of trade secrets or other information the disclosure of which the manager in good faith believes is not in the best interest of the limited liability company or could damage the limited liability company or its business or which the limited liability company is required by law or by agreement with a third party to keep confidential.

(5) A limited liability company may maintain its records in other than a written form if such form is capable of conversion into written form within a reasonable time.

(6) Any action to enforce any right arising under this section shall be brought in the appropriate circuit court.

History.—

s. 16, ch. 93-284; s. 1, ch. 99-315; s. 8, ch. 2002-272.

608.411 Amendments to or restatements of articles of organization.—

(1) The articles of organization of a limited liability company are amended by filing the articles of amendment thereto with the Department of State. The articles of amendment shall set forth:

(a) The name of the limited liability company.

(b) The date of filing of the articles of organization.

(c) The amendment to the articles of organization.

(2) Unless otherwise provided in this chapter or in the articles of amendment, the articles of amendment shall be effective when filed with the Department of State.

(3) A limited liability company may, whenever desired, integrate into a single instrument all provisions of its articles of organization then in effect and it may at the same time further amend its articles of organization by adopting restated articles of organization which meet all the requirements of s. 608.407.

(4) If the restated articles of organization merely restate and integrate but do not further amend the then-effective articles of organization, the limited liability company shall title the filing "Restated Articles of Organization," together with such other words as the limited liability company deems appropriate. If the restated articles restate and integrate and also further amend in any respect the then-effective articles of

organization, the limited liability company shall title the filing "Amended and Restated Articles of Organization," together with such other words as the limited liability company deems appropriate. In each case described in this subsection, the document shall be executed as provided in this chapter for articles of organization and filed as provided by this chapter with the Department of State.

(5) Restated articles of organization shall state, either in their heading or in an introductory paragraph, the limited liability company's present name, and, if it has been changed, the name under which it was originally filed; the date of filing of its original articles of organization with the Department of State; and any future effective date or time if other than the date and time of the filing of the restated articles of organization. Restated articles of organization shall also state that they were duly executed and are being filed in accordance with this section. If the restated articles of organization only restate and integrate and do not further amend the limited liability company's articles of organization as theretofore amended or supplemented and there is no discrepancy between those provisions and the restated articles of organization, they shall state that fact as well.

(6) Upon the filing of the restated articles of organization with the Department of State, or upon any future effective date or time provided in restated articles of organization, the articles of organization existing prior to such filing shall be superseded and the restated articles of organization, including any further amendment or changes made thereby, shall become the limited liability company's articles of organization. The original effective date of the limited liability company's formation shall remain unchanged.

(7) Any amendment or change effected in connection with the restatement and integration of the articles of organization shall be subject to any other provisions of this chapter, not inconsistent with this section, which would apply if separate articles of amendment were filed to effect such amendment or change.

History.—
s. 2, ch. 82-177; s. 58, ch. 83-216; s. 17, ch. 93-284; s. 1, ch. 99-315; s. 9, ch. 2002-272.

608.4115 Correcting the articles of organization filed of record.—

(1) A limited liability company or foreign limited liability company may correct the articles of organization filed of record with the Department of State within 30 business days after filing if the record contains a false or erroneous statement or was defectively signed.

(2) The articles of organization filed of record are corrected:

(a) By preparing articles of correction that:

1. Describe the articles of organization filed of record, including their filing date, or attach a copy of the articles of organization to the articles of correction.

2. Specify the incorrect statement and the reason the statement is incorrect or the manner in which the signing was defective.

3. Correct the incorrect statement or defective signing.

(b) By delivering the articles of correction to the Department of State for filing.

(3) The articles of correction are effective retroactively to the effective date of the articles of organization they correct except as to persons relying on the uncorrected articles of organization and adversely affected by the correction. As to those persons, the articles of correction are effective when filed.

History.—
s. 1, ch. 99-315.

608.415 Registered office and registered agent.—

(1) Each limited liability company shall have and continuously maintain in this state:

(a) A registered office, which may be the same as its place of business; and

(b) A registered agent, which agent may be either:

1. An individual who resides in this state whose business office is identical with such registered office.

2. A foreign or domestic entity authorized to transact business in this state, having a business office identical with such registered office.

(2) A registered agent or a successor registered agent appointed pursuant to s. 608.416 on whom process may be served shall each file a statement in writing with the Department of State accepting the appointment as registered agent simultaneously with being designated. Such statement or acceptance shall state that the registered agent is familiar with, and accepts, the obligations of that position as provided for in this chapter.

(3) The Department of State shall maintain an accurate record of the registered agents and registered office for the service of process and shall furnish any information disclosed thereby promptly upon request and payment of the required fee.

(4) A limited liability company may not prosecute, maintain, or defend any action in any court until the limited liability company complies with the provisions of this section and pays to the Department of State a penalty of $5 for each day it has failed to comply or $500, whichever amount is less, and pays any other amount required under this chapter.

History.—
s. 2, ch. 82-177; s. 59, ch. 83-216; s. 19, ch. 93-284; s. 1, ch. 99-315.

608.416 Change of registered office or registered agent.—

(1) A limited liability company may change its registered office or agent by filing with the Department of State a statement setting forth:

(a) The name of the limited liability company.

(b) The street address of its current registered office.

(c) If the street address of its registered office is to be changed, the new street address.

(d) If its current registered agent is to be changed, the name of the new registered agent and the new registered agent's written consent to the appointment, either on the statement or attached to it.

(e) That such change was authorized by affirmative vote of the members or as otherwise provided in the articles of organization or the operating agreement of the limited liability company.

(2) Any registered agent may resign his or her agency appointment by signing and delivering for filing with the Department of State a statement of resignation and mailing a copy of such statement to the limited liability company at its principal office address shown in its most recently filed document. The agency is terminated and the registered office discontinued, if so provided, on the 31st day after the date on which the statement was filed with the Department of State. After receipt of the notice of the resignation of its registered agent, the limited liability company for which such registered agent was acting shall obtain and designate a new registered agent, to take the place of the resigning registered agent.

(3) A registered agent may change the address of the registered office of any limited liability company for which such agent is the registered agency by notifying the limited liability company in writing of the change, signing, either manually or in facsimile, and delivering to the Department of State for filing a statement that complies with the requirements of paragraphs (1)(a)-(d), and reciting that the limited liability company has been notified of the change.

History.—
s. 2, ch. 82-177; s. 60, ch. 83-216; s. 20, ch. 93-284; s. 49, ch. 97-102; s. 1, ch. 99-315.

608.4211 Contributions to capital and liability for contribution.—
(1)   The contribution of a member may be in cash, property, or services rendered, or a promissory note or other obligation to contribute cash or property or to perform services.
(2)   A promise by a member to contribute to the limited liability company is not enforceable unless it is set out in writing signed by the member.
(3)   Unless otherwise provided in the articles of organization or operating agreement, a member is obligated to the limited liability company to perform any enforceable promise to contribute cash or property or to perform services, even if the member is unable to perform because of the member's death or disability or any other reason. If a member does not make the required contribution of property or services, the member is obligated, at the option of the limited liability company, to contribute cash equal to that portion of the agreed value, as stated in the records of the limited liability company required to be kept pursuant to this chapter, of the stated contribution that has not been made. The foregoing option shall be in addition to, and not in lieu of, any other rights, including the right to specific performance, that the limited liability company may have against such member under the articles of organization or operating agreement or applicable law.
(4)   Unless otherwise provided in the articles of organization or the operating agreement, the obligation of a member to make a contribution or return money or other property paid or distributed in violation of this chapter may be compromised only by consent of all the members. Notwithstanding the compromise, the creditor of a limited liability company, who extends credit or otherwise acts in reasonable reliance upon that obligation after the member has signed a writing that indicates the obligation and before the amendment or cancellation of the writing to indicate the compromise, may enforce the original obligation to the extent the creditor relied on the obligation when extending credit.
(5)   The articles of organization or operating agreement of a limited liability company may provide that the interest of any member who fails to make any contribution that the member is obligated to make shall be subject to specified penalties for, or specified consequences of, such failure. Such penalties or consequences may take the form of reducing the defaulting member's proportionate membership interest in the limited liability company, subordinating the defaulting member's interest in the limited liability company to that of the nondefaulting members, a forced sale of the defaulting member's membership interest, the forfeiture of the defaulting member's membership interest, the lending by other members of the amount necessary to meet the defaulting member's commitment, a fixing of the value of the defaulting member's membership interest by appraisal or by formula and redemption or sale of the defaulting member's membership interest at such value, or other penalties or consequences.
History.—
s. 2, ch. 82-177; s. 21, ch. 93-284; s. 50, ch. 97-102; s. 1, ch. 99-315.

608.422   Management of the limited liability company.—
(1)   Unless otherwise provided in its articles of organization or the operating agreement, the limited liability company shall be a member-managed company.
(2)   In a member-managed company, unless otherwise provided in its articles of organization or operating agreement:
(a)   Management shall be vested in its members or elected managing members in proportion to the then-current percentage or other interest of members in the profits of the limited liability company owned by all of the members or elected managing members.

(b)   Except as otherwise provided in subsection (3) or in this chapter, the decision of a majority-in-interest of the members or elected managing members shall be controlling.
(3)   If the articles of organization or the operating agreement provide for the management of the limited liability company by a manager or managers, the management of the limited liability company shall be vested in a manager or managers and the limited liability company shall be a manager-managed company.
(4)   In a manager-managed company, unless otherwise provided in its articles of organization or operating agreement:
(a)   Each manager has equal rights in the management and conduct of the limited liability company's business.
(b)   Except as otherwise provided in subsection (3) or in this chapter, any matter relating to the business of the limited liability company may be exclusively decided by the manager or, if there is more than one manager, by a majority of the managers.
(c)   A manager:
1.   Must be designated, appointed, elected, removed, or replaced by a vote, approval, or consent of a majority-in-interest of the members; and
2.   Holds office until a successor has been elected and qualified, unless the manager sooner resigns or is removed.
(5)   Action requiring the consent of members or managers under this chapter may be taken without a meeting, subject to the limitations of s. 608.4231.
(6)   Unless otherwise provided in the articles of organization or operating agreement, a member, managing member, or manager may appoint a proxy to vote or otherwise act for the member, managing member, or manager by signing an appointment instrument, either personally or by the member's, managing member's, or manager's attorney-in-fact.
(7)   Unless otherwise provided in the articles of organization or operating agreement, a member, managing member, or manager may also hold the offices and have such other responsibilities accorded to thcm by the members and set out in the articles of organization or the operating agreement of the limited liability company.
History.—
s. 2, ch. 82-177; s. 22, ch. 93-284; s. 1, ch. 99-315; s. 10, ch. 2002-272.

608.4225   General standards for managers and managing members.—
(1)   Subject to ss. 608.4226 and 608.423, each manager and managing member shall owe a duty of loyalty and a duty of care to the limited liability company and all of the members of the limited liability company.
(a)   Subject to s. 608.4226, the duty of loyalty is limited to:
1.   Accounting to the limited liability company and holding as trustee for the limited liability company any property, profit, or benefit derived by such manager or managing member in the conduct or winding up of the limited liability company business or derived from a use by such manager or managing member of limited liability company property, including the appropriation of a limited liability company opportunity.
2.   Refraining from dealing with the limited liability company in the conduct or winding up of the limited liability company business as or on behalf of a party having an interest adverse to the limited liability company.
3.   Refraining from competing with the limited liability company in the conduct of the limited liability company business before the dissolution of the limited liability company.
(b)   The duty of care is limited to refraining from engaging in grossly negligent or reckless conduct, intentional misconduct, or a knowing violation of law.
(c)   Each manager and managing member shall discharge the duties to the limited liability company and its members under

this chapter or under the articles of organization or operating agreement and exercise any rights consistent with the obligation of good faith and fair dealing.

(d) A manager or managing member does not violate a duty or obligation under this chapter or under the articles of organization or operating agreement merely because the manager's or managing member's conduct furthers such manager's or managing member's own interest.

(e) A manager or managing member may lend money to and transact other business with the limited liability company. As to each loan or transaction, the rights and obligations of the manager or managing member are the same as those of a person who is not a member, subject to other applicable law.

(f) This section applies to a person winding up the limited liability company business as the personal or other legal representative of the last surviving member as if such person were a manager or managing member.

(2) In discharging a manager's or managing member's duties, a manager or managing member is entitled to rely on information, opinions, reports, or statements, including financial statements and other financial data, if prepared or presented by:

(a) One or more members or employees of the limited liability company whom the manager or managing member reasonably believes to be reliable and competent in the matters presented;

(b) Legal counsel, public accountants, or other persons as to matters the manager or managing member reasonably believes are within the persons' professional or expert competence; or

(c) A committee of managers, members, or managing members of which the affected manager or managing member is not a participant if the manager or managing member reasonably believes the committee merits confidence.

(3) In discharging a manager's or managing member's duties, a manager or managing member may consider such factors as the manager or managing member deems relevant, including the long-term prospects and interests of the limited liability company and its members, and the social, economic, legal, or other effects of any action on the employees, suppliers, customers of the limited liability company, the communities and society in which the limited liability company operates, and the economy of the state and the nation.

(4) A member, manager, or managing member is not acting in good faith if the member, manager, or managing member has knowledge concerning the matter in question that makes reliance otherwise permitted by subsection (2) unwarranted.

(5) A manager or managing member is not liable for any action taken as a manager or managing member, or any failure to take any action, if the manager or managing member performed the duties of the manager's or managing member's position in compliance with this section.

History.—

s. 23, ch. 93-284; s. 51, ch. 97-102; s. 1, ch. 99-315; s. 11, ch. 2002-272; s. 5, ch. 2005-267.

608.4226 Conflicts of interest.—

(1) No contract or other transaction between a limited liability company and one or more of its members, managers, or managing members or any other limited liability company, corporation, firm, association, or entity in which one or more of its members, managers, or managing members are managers, managing members, directors, or officers or are financially interested shall be either void or voidable because of such relationship or interest, because such members, managers, or managing members are present at the meeting of the members, managers, or managing members or a committee thereof which authorizes, approves, or ratifies such contract or transaction, or because their votes are counted for such purpose, if:

(a) The fact of such relationship or interest is disclosed or known to the managers or managing members or committee which authorizes, approves, or ratifies the contract or transaction by a vote or consent sufficient for the purpose without counting the votes or consents of such interested members, managers, or managing members;

(b) The fact of such relationship or interest is disclosed or known to the members entitled to vote and they authorize, approve, or ratify such contract or transaction by vote or written consent; or

(c) The contract or transaction is fair and reasonable as to the limited liability company at the time it is authorized by the managers, managing members, a committee, or the members.

(2) For purposes of paragraph (1)(a) only, a conflict of interest transaction is authorized, approved, or ratified if it receives the affirmative vote of a majority of the managers or managing members, or of the committee, who have no relationship or interest in the transaction described in subsection (1), but a transaction may not be authorized, approved, or ratified under this section by a single manager of a manager-managed company or a single managing member of a member-managed company, unless the company is a single member limited liability company. If a majority of the managers or managing members who have no such relationship or interest in the transaction vote to authorize, approve, or ratify the transaction, a quorum is present for the purpose of taking action under this section. The presence of, or a vote cast by, a manager or managing member with such relationship or interest in the transaction does not affect the validity of any action taken under paragraph (1)(a) if the transaction is otherwise authorized, approved, or ratified as provided in that subsection, but such presence or vote of those managers or managing members may be counted for purposes of determining whether the transaction is approved under other sections of this chapter.

(3) For purposes of paragraph (1)(b) only, a conflict of interest transaction is authorized, approved, or ratified if it receives the vote of a majority-in-interest of the members entitled to be counted under this subsection. Membership interests owned by or voted under the control of a manager or managing member who has a relationship or interest in the transaction described in subsection (1) may not be counted in a vote of members to determine whether to authorize, approve, or ratify a conflict of interest transaction under paragraph (1)(b). The vote of those membership interests, however, is counted in determining whether the transaction is approved under other sections of this act. A majority-in-interest of the members, whether or not present, that are entitled to be counted in a vote on the transaction under this subsection constitutes a quorum for the purpose of taking action under this section.

History.—

s. 1, ch. 99-315; s. 12, ch. 2002-272.

608.4227 Liability of members, managing members, and managers.—

(1) Except as provided in this chapter, the members, managers, and managing members of a limited liability company are not liable, solely by reason of being a member or serving as a manager or managing member, under a judgment, decree, or order of a court, or in any other manner, for a debt, obligation, or liability of the limited liability company;

(2) Any such member, managing member, manager, or other person acting under the articles of organization or operating agreement of a limited liability company is not liable to the limited liability company or to any such other member, managing member, or manager for the member's, managing member's, manager's, or other person's good faith reliance on the provisions of the limited liability company's articles of organization or operating agreement; and

(3)   The member's, managing member's, manager's, or other person's duties and liabilities may be expanded or restricted by provisions in a limited liability company's articles of organization or operating agreement.

History.—

s. 2, ch. 82-177; s. 36, ch. 93-284; s. 1, ch. 99-315; s. 13, ch. 2002-272.

Note.—

Former s. 608.436.

608.4228   Limitation of liability of managers and managing members.—

(1)   A manager or a managing member shall not be personally liable for monetary damages to the limited liability company, its members, or any other person for any statement, vote, decision, or failure to act regarding management or policy decisions by a manager or a managing member, unless:

(a)   The manager or managing member breached or failed to perform the duties as a manager or managing member; and

(b)   The manager's or managing member's breach of, or failure to perform, those duties constitutes any of the following:

1.   A violation of the criminal law, unless the manager or managing member had a reasonable cause to believe his or her conduct was lawful or had no reasonable cause to believe such conduct was unlawful. A judgment or other final adjudication against a manager or managing member in any criminal proceeding for a violation of the criminal law estops that manager or managing member from contesting the fact that such breach, or failure to perform, constitutes a violation of the criminal law, but does not estop the manager or managing member from establishing that he or she had reasonable cause to believe that his or her conduct was lawful or had no reasonable cause to believe that such conduct was unlawful.

2.   A transaction from which the manager or managing member derived an improper personal benefit, either directly or indirectly.

3.   A distribution in violation of s. 608.426.

4.   In a proceeding by or in the right of the limited liability company to procure a judgment in its favor or by or in the right of a member, conscious disregard of the best interest of the limited liability company, or willful misconduct.

5.   In a proceeding by or in the right of someone other than the limited liability company or a member, recklessness or an act or omission which was committed in bad faith or with malicious purpose or in a manner exhibiting wanton and willful disregard of human rights, safety, or property.

(2)   For the purposes of this section, the term "recklessness" means acting, or failing to act, in conscious disregard of a risk known, or so obvious that it should have been known, to the manager or managing member, and known to the manager or managing member, or so obvious that it should have been known, to be so great as to make it highly probable that harm would follow from such action or failure to act.

(3)   A manager or managing member is deemed not to have derived an improper personal benefit from any transaction if the transaction and the nature of any personal benefit derived by the manager or managing member are not prohibited by state or federal law or the articles of organization or operating agreement and, without further limitation, the transaction and the nature of any personal benefit derived by a manager or managing member are disclosed or known to the members, and the transaction was authorized, approved, or ratified by the vote of a majority-in-interest of the members other than the managing member, or the transaction was fair and reasonable to the limited liability company at the time it was authorized by the manager or managing member, notwithstanding that a manager or managing member received a personal benefit.

(4)   The circumstances set forth in subsection (3) are not exclusive and do not preclude the existence of other circumstances under which a manager will be deemed not to have derived an improper benefit.

History.—

s. 37, ch. 93-284; s. 58, ch. 97-102; s. 1, ch. 99-315; s. 14, ch. 2002-272.

Note.—

Former s. 608.4362.

608.4229   Indemnification of members, managers, managing members, officers, employees, and agents.—

(1)   Subject to such standards and restrictions, if any, as are set forth in its articles of organization or operating agreement, a limited liability company may, and shall have the power to, but shall not be required to, indemnify and hold harmless any member or manager or other person from and against any and all claims and demands whatsoever.

(2)   Notwithstanding subsection (1), indemnification or advancement of expenses shall not be made to or on behalf of any member, manager, managing member, officer, employee, or agent if a judgment or other final adjudication establishes that the actions, or omissions to act, of such member, manager, managing member, officer, employee, or agent were material to the cause of action so adjudicated and constitute any of the following:

(a)   A violation of criminal law, unless the member, manager, managing member, officer, employee, or agent had no reasonable cause to believe such conduct was unlawful.

(b)   A transaction from which the member, manager, managing member, officer, employee, or agent derived an improper personal benefit.

(c)   In the case of a manager or managing member, a circumstance under which the liability provisions of s. 608.426 are applicable.

(d)   Willful misconduct or a conscious disregard for the best interests of the limited liability company in a proceeding by or in the right of the limited liability company to procure a judgment in its favor or in a proceeding by or in the right of a member.

History.—

s. 38, ch. 93-284; s. 59, ch. 97-102; s. 1, ch. 99-315; s. 15, ch. 2002-272.

Note.—

Former s. 608.4363.

608.423   Limited liability company operating agreement; nonwaivable provisions.—

(1)   Except as otherwise provided in subsection (2), all members of a limited liability company may enter into an operating agreement, which need not be in writing, to regulate the affairs of the limited liability company and the conduct of its business, establish duties in addition to those set forth in this chapter, and to govern relations among the members, managers, and company. Any inconsistency between written and oral operating agreements shall be resolved in favor of the written agreement. The members of a limited liability company may enter into an operating agreement before, after, or at the time the articles of organization are filed, and the operating agreement takes effect on the date of the formation of the limited liability company or on any other date provided in the operating agreement. To the extent the operating agreement does not otherwise provide, this chapter governs relations among the members, managers, and limited liability company.

(2)   The operating agreement may not:

(a)   Unreasonably restrict a right to information or access to records under s. 608.4101;

(b)   Eliminate the duty of loyalty under s. 608.4225, but the agreement may:

1. Identify specific types or categories of activities that do not violate the duty of loyalty, if not manifestly unreasonable; and

2. Specify the number or percentage of members or disinterested managers that may authorize or ratify, after full disclosure of all material facts, a specific act or transaction that otherwise would violate the duty of loyalty;

(c) Unreasonably reduce the duty of care under s. 608.4225;

(d) Eliminate the obligation of good faith and fair dealing under s. 608.4225, but the operating agreement may determine the standards by which the performance of the obligation is to be measured, if the standards are not manifestly unreasonable;

(e) Vary the requirement to wind up the limited liability company's business in a case specified in this chapter; or

(f) Restrict rights of a person, other than a manager, member, or transferee of a member's distributional interest, under this chapter.

(3) The power to adopt, alter, amend, or repeal the operating agreement of a limited liability company shall be vested in the members of the limited liability company unless vested in the manager or managers of the limited liability company by the articles of organization or operating agreement, provided that any amendment to a written operating agreement shall be in writing. The operating agreement adopted by the members or by the manager or managers may be repealed or altered; a new operating agreement may be adopted by the members; and the members may prescribe in any operating agreement made by them that such operating agreement may not be altered, amended, or repealed by the manager or managers.

(4) Unless the articles of organization or the operating agreement provides otherwise, if the management of the limited liability company is vested in a manager or managers, the managers may adopt an operating agreement to be effective only in an emergency as defined in subsection (7). The emergency operating agreement, which is subject to amendment or repeal by the members, may make all provisions necessary for managing the limited liability company during an emergency, including procedures for calling a meeting of the managers and designation of additional or substitute managers.

(5) All provisions of the regular operating agreement consistent with the emergency regulations remain effective during the emergency. The emergency operating agreement is not effective after the emergency ends.

(6) Actions taken by the limited liability company in good faith in accordance with the emergency operating agreement have the effect of binding the limited liability company and may not be used to impose liability on a manager, employee, or agent of the limited liability company.

(7) An emergency exists for purposes of this section if the limited liability company's managers cannot readily be assembled because of some catastrophic event.

History.—

s. 2, ch. 82-177; s. 61, ch. 83-216; s. 24, ch. 93-284; s. 1, ch. 99-315; s. 16, ch. 2002-272.

608.4231 Voting by members and managers.—

(1) The articles of organization or operating agreement may provide for classes or groups of members having such relative rights, powers, and duties as the articles of organization or operating agreement may provide, and may make provision for the future creation in the manner provided in the articles of organization or operating agreement of additional classes or groups of members having such relative rights, powers, and duties as may from time to time be established, including rights, powers, and duties senior to existing classes and groups of members. The articles of organization or operating agreement may provide for the taking of an action, including the amendment of the articles of organization or operating agree-

ment, without the vote or approval of any member or class or group of members, including an action to create under the provisions of the articles of organization or operating agreement a class or group of limited liability company interests that was not previously outstanding. The articles of organization or operating agreement may provide that any member or class or group of members shall have no voting rights.

(2) The articles of organization or operating agreement may grant to all or certain identified members or a specified class or group of the members the right to vote separately or with all or any class or group of the members or manager on any matter. Voting by members may be on a per capita, number, financial interest, class, group, or any other basis.

(3) If no conflicting voting provision is contained in the articles of organization or operating agreement:

(a) The members of a limited liability company shall vote in proportion to their then-current percentage or other allocable interest in the profits of the limited liability company or, in the case of a member who has assigned the member's entire economic interest in the limited liability company to a person who has not been admitted as a member, in proportion to the then-current percentage or other allocable interest in the profits of the limited liability company that the assigning member would have, had the assignment not been made.

(b) In all matters in which a vote is required, a vote of a majority-in-interest of the members shall be sufficient unless provided otherwise in the limited liability company's articles of organization or operating agreement or this chapter.

(4) Notwithstanding any provision to the contrary in the articles of organization or operating agreement, in no event shall the articles of organization be amended by a vote of less than a majority-in-interest of the members.

(5) Notwithstanding any provision to the contrary in the articles of organization or operating agreement, members shall have the right to vote on a dissolution of the limited liability company as provided in s. 608.441 and on a merger of the limited liability company as provided in s. 608.4381.

(6) Except as otherwise provided in the articles of organization or the operating agreement, if the members have appointed more than one manager or managing member to manage the business of the limited liability company, decisions of the managers or managing members shall be made by majority vote of the managers or managing members if at a meeting, or by unanimous written consent. Unless otherwise provided in the articles of organization or operating agreement, on any matter that is to be voted on by one or more managers or managing members, the managers or managing members may vote in person or by proxy. Within 10 days after obtaining such authorization by written consent, notice must be given to those managers or managing members who have not consented in writing or who are not entitled to vote on the action.

(7) The articles of organization or operating agreement which grants a right to vote may set forth provisions relating to notice of the time, place, or purpose of any meeting at which any matter is to be voted on by any members, waiver of any such notice, action by consent without a meeting, the establishment of a record date, quorum requirements, voting in person or by proxy, or any other matter with respect to the exercise of any such right to vote.

(8) Unless otherwise provided in the articles of organization or operating agreement, on any matter that is to be voted on by members, the members may take such action without a meeting, without prior notice, and without a vote if a consent or consents in writing, setting forth the action so taken, are signed by the members having not less than the minimum number of votes that would be necessary to authorize or take such action at a meeting, but in no event by a vote of less than a majority-in-interest of the members that would be necessary

to authorize or take such action at a meeting. Unless otherwise provided in the articles of organization or operating agreement, on any matter that is to be voted on by members, the members may vote in person or by proxy. Within 10 days after obtaining such authorization by written consent, notice must be given to those members who have not consented in writing or who are not entitled to vote on the action.

History.—

s. 25, ch. 93-284; s. 1, ch. 99-315; s. 17, ch. 2002-272.

608.4232 Admission of additional members.—

Except as otherwise provided in the articles of organization or the operating agreement, no person may be admitted as a member unless a majority-in-interest of the members consent in writing to the admission of the additional member.

History.—

s. 26, ch. 93-284; s. 1, ch. 99-315.

608.4235 Agency of members and managers or managing members.—

(1)   Subject to subsections (2) and (3):

(a)   In a member-managed company, each member is an agent of the limited liability company for the purpose of its business, and an act of a member, including the signing of an instrument in the limited liability company's name, for apparently carrying on in the ordinary course the limited liability company's business or business of the kind carried on by the company binds the limited liability company, unless the member had no authority to act for the limited liability company in the particular matter and the person with whom the member was dealing knew or had notice that the member lacked authority.

(b)   An act of a member which is not apparently for carrying on in the ordinary course the limited liability company's business or business of the kind carried on by the limited liability company binds the limited liability company only if the act was authorized by appropriate vote of the other members.

(2)   Subject to subsection (3), in a manager-managed company:

(a)   A member is not an agent of the limited liability company for the purpose of its business solely by reason of being a member. Each manager is an agent of the limited liability company for the purpose of its business, and an act of a manager, including the signing of an instrument in the limited liability company's name, for apparently carrying on in the ordinary course the limited liability company's business or business of the kind carried on by the company binds the limited liability company, unless the manager had no authority to act for the limited liability company in the particular matter and the person with whom the manager was dealing knew or had notice that the manager lacked authority.

(b)   An act of a manager which is not apparently for carrying on in the ordinary course the limited liability company's business or business of the kind carried on by the limited liability company binds the limited liability company only if the act was authorized under s. 608.422.

(3)   Unless the articles of organization or operating agreement limit the authority of a member, any member of a member-managed company or manager of a manager-managed company may sign and deliver any instrument transferring or affecting the limited liability company's interest in real property. The instrument is conclusive in favor of a person who gives value without knowledge of the lack of the authority of the person signing and delivering the instrument.

History.—

s. 1, ch. 99-315; s. 18, ch. 2002-272.

608.4236 Delegation of rights and powers to manage.—

Unless otherwise provided in the limited liability company's articles of organization or operating agreement, a member or manager of a limited liability company has the power and authority to delegate to one or more other persons the member's or manager's, as the case may be, rights and powers to manage and control the business and affairs of the limited liability company, including the power and authority to delegate to agents, boards of managers, managing members or directors, officers and assistant officers, and employees of a member or manager of the limited liability company, and the power and authority to delegate by a management agreement or another agreement with, or otherwise, to other persons. Unless otherwise provided in the limited liability company's articles of organization or operating agreement, such delegation by a member or manager of a limited liability company shall not cause the member or manager to cease to be a member or manager, as the case may be, of the limited liability company.

History.—

s. 1, ch. 99-315.

608.4237 Membership termination upon events of bankruptcy.—

A person ceases to be a member of a limited liability company upon the occurrence of any of the following:

(1)   Unless otherwise provided in the articles of organization or operating agreement, or with the written consent of all members, a member:

(a)   Makes an assignment for the benefit of creditors;

(b)   Files a voluntary petition in bankruptcy;

(c)   Is adjudged a bankrupt or insolvent, or has entered against the member an order for relief, in any bankruptcy or insolvency proceeding;

(d)   Files a petition or answer seeking for herself or himself any reorganization, arrangement, composition, readjustment, liquidation, dissolution, or similar relief under any statute, law, or regulation;

(e)   Files an answer or other pleading admitting or failing to contest the material allegations of a petition filed against the member in any proceeding of this nature; or

(f)   Seeks, consents to, or acquiesces in the appointment of a trustee, receiver, or liquidator of the member or of all or any substantial part of the member's properties; or

(2)   Unless otherwise provided in the articles of organization or operating agreement, or with the written consent of all members, 120 days after the commencement of any proceeding against the member seeking reorganization, arrangement, composition, readjustment, liquidation, dissolution, or similar relief under any statute, law, or regulation, if the proceeding has not been dismissed, or if within 90 days after the appointment without the member's consent or acquiescence of a trustee, receiver, or liquidator of the member or of all or any substantial part of the member's properties, the appointment is not vacated or stayed, or within 90 days after the expiration of any such stay, the appointment is not vacated.

History.—

s. 1, ch. 99-315; s. 12, ch. 2000-159.

608.4238 Unauthorized assumption of powers.—

All persons purporting to act as or on behalf of a limited liability company, having actual knowledge that there was no organization of a limited liability company under this chapter, are jointly and severally liable for all liabilities created while so acting except for any liability to any person who also had actual knowledge that there was no organization of a limited liability company.

History.—

s. 2, ch. 82-177; s. 1, ch. 99-315; s. 19, ch. 2002-272.

Note.—

Former s. 608.437.

608.425 Limited liability company property.—

(1)   All property originally contributed to the limited liability company or subsequently acquired by a limited liability company by purchase or otherwise is limited liability company property.

(2)   Unless otherwise provided in the articles of organization or the operating agreement, property acquired with limited liability company funds is limited liability company property.
(3)   Instruments and documents providing for the acquisition, mortgage, or disposition of property of the limited liability company shall be valid and binding upon the limited liability company, if they are executed in accordance with this chapter.
History.—
s. 2, ch. 82-177; s. 62, ch. 83-216; s. 28, ch. 93-284; s. 1, ch. 99-315; s. 20, ch. 2002-272.

608.426   Distributions; impairment of capital.—
(1)   The limited liability company may make distributions to its members in accordance with the provisions contained in the operating agreement, except that no distribution may be made if after the distribution the limited liability company would be insolvent. If the operating agreement does not provide for the payment of distributions to members, the distributions shall be made on the basis of the agreed value, as stated in the records of the limited liability company, of the contributions made by each member to the extent they have been received by the limited liability company and have not been returned.
(2)   The managers or managing members of a limited liability company may base a determination that a distribution is not prohibited under subsection (1) either on financial statements prepared on the basis of accounting practices and principles that are reasonable in the circumstances or on a fair valuation or other method that is reasonable in the circumstances. In the case of any distribution based upon such financial statement or such a valuation, each such distribution shall be identified as a distribution based upon such financial statements or a fair valuation of assets, and the amount distributed shall be disclosed to the receiving members concurrent with their receipt of the distribution.
(3)   A manager or managing member who votes for or assents to a distribution made in violation of this section, the articles of incorporation, or the operating agreement, is personally liable to the limited liability company for the amount of the distribution that exceeds what could have been distributed without such violation if it is established that the manager or managing member did not perform the manager's or managing member's duties in compliance with s. 608.4225. In any proceeding commenced under this section, a manager or managing member has all of the defenses ordinarily available to a manager or managing member.
(4)   A manager or managing member held liable under subsection (3) for an unlawful distribution is entitled to contribution:
(a)   From every other manager or managing member who is also liable under subsection (3) for the unlawful distribution; and
(b)   From each member to the extent of the amount the member accepted knowing the distribution was made in violation of this section, the articles of incorporation, or the operating agreement.
(5)   A proceeding under this section is barred unless it is commenced within 2 years after the date on which the distribution was made. In the case of a distribution in the form of indebtedness, each payment of principal or interest is treated as a distribution.
History.—
s. 2, ch. 82-177; s. 40, ch. 83-215; s. 29, ch. 93-284; s. 52, ch. 97-102; s. 1, ch. 99-315.

608.4261   Sharing of profits and losses.—
The profits and losses of the limited liability company shall be allocated among the members in the manner provided in the articles of organization or the operating agreement. If the articles of organization do not or the operating agreement does not provide for the allocation of profits and losses

among members, profits and losses shall be allocated on the basis of the agreed value, as stated in the records of the limited liability company, of the contributions made by each member to the extent such contributions have been received by the limited liability company and have not been returned.
History.—
s. 30, ch. 93-284; s. 1, ch. 99-315.

608.427   Withdrawal of member and distribution upon withdrawal.—
(1)   A member may withdraw from a limited liability company only at the time or upon the occurrence of an event specified in the articles of organization or operating agreement and in accordance with the articles of organization or operating agreement. Notwithstanding anything to the contrary under applicable law, unless the articles of organization or operating agreement provides otherwise, a member may not resign from a limited liability company prior to the dissolution and winding up of the limited liability company. Notwithstanding anything to the contrary under applicable law, the articles of organization or operating agreement may provide that a limited liability company interest may not be assigned prior to the dissolution and winding up of the limited liability company.
(2)   Upon withdrawal, a withdrawing member is entitled to receive any distribution to which the withdrawing member is entitled under the articles of organization or operating agreement, and, if not otherwise provided in the articles of organization and operating agreement, the withdrawing member is entitled to receive, within a reasonable time after withdrawal, the fair value of the withdrawing member's interest in the limited liability company as of the date of resignation based upon the withdrawing member's right to share in distributions from the limited liability company.
(3)   In the absence of a statement in the articles of organization or the operating agreement to the contrary or the consent of all members of the limited liability company, a member, irrespective of the nature of the member's contribution, has only the right to demand and receive cash in return for the member's contribution to capital.
History.—
s. 2, ch. 82-177; s. 31, ch. 93-284; s. 53, ch. 97-102; s. 1, ch. 99-315.

608.428   Liability upon wrongful distribution.—
(1)   If a member receives a distribution in violation of the articles of organization, the operating agreement, or this chapter, the member is liable to the limited liability company for a period of 3 years thereafter for the amount of the distribution wrongfully made.
(2)   A member may not receive a distribution from a limited liability company to the extent that, after giving effect to the distribution, the limited liability company would be insolvent.
History.—
s. 32, ch. 93-284; s. 54, ch. 97-102; s. 1, ch. 99-315; s. 21, ch. 2002-272.

608.431   Nature of interest of member in limited liability company.—
An interest of a member in a limited liability company is personal property.
History.—
s. 2, ch. 82-177.

608.432   Assignment of member's interest.—
(1)   A limited liability company interest is assignable in whole or in part except as provided in the articles of organization or operating agreement. The assignee of a member's interest shall have no right to participate in the management of the business and affairs of a limited liability company except as provided in the articles of organization or operating agreement and upon:

(a)   The approval of all of the members of the limited liability company other than the member assigning the limited liability company interest; or

(b)   Compliance with any procedure provided for in the articles of organization or operating agreement.

(2)   Unless otherwise provided in the articles of organization or operating agreement:

(a)   An assignment of a membership interest does not entitle the assignee to become or to exercise any rights or powers of a member;

(b)   An assignment of a membership interest entitles the assignee to share in such profits and losses, to receive such distribution or distributions, and to receive such allocation of income, gain, loss, deduction, or credit or similar item to which the assignor was entitled, to the extent assigned; and

(c)   A member ceases to be a member and to have the power to exercise any rights or powers of a member upon assignment of all of the membership interest of such member. Unless otherwise provided in the articles of organization or operating agreement, the pledge of, or granting of a security interest, lien, or other encumbrance in or against, any or all of the membership interest of a member shall not cause the member to cease to be a member or to have the power to exercise any rights or powers of a member.

(3)   The articles of organization or operating agreement may provide that a member's interest in a limited liability company may be evidenced by a certificate of membership interest issued by the limited liability company.

(4)   Unless otherwise provided in the articles of organization or operating agreement and except to the extent assumed by agreement, until an assignee of a membership interest becomes a member, the assignee shall have no liability as a member solely as a result of the assignment.

(5)   Unless otherwise provided in the articles of organization or operating agreement, a limited liability company may acquire, by purchase, redemption, or otherwise, any membership interest or other interest of a member or manager in the limited liability company. Unless otherwise provided in the articles of organization or operating agreement, any such interest so acquired by the limited liability company shall be deemed canceled.

History.—

s. 2, ch. 82-177; s. 33, ch. 93-284; s. 55, ch. 97-102; s. 1, ch. 99-315; s. 22, ch. 2002-272.

608.433   Right of assignee to become member.—

(1)   Unless otherwise provided in the articles of organization or operating agreement, an assignee of a limited liability company interest may become a member only if all members other than the member assigning the interest consent.

(2)   An assignee who has become a member has, to the extent assigned, the rights and powers, and is subject to the restrictions and liabilities, of the assigning member under the articles of organization, the operating agreement, and this chapter. An assignee who becomes a member also is liable for the obligations of the assignee's assignor to make and return contributions as provided in s. 608.4211 and wrongful distributions as provided in s. 608.428. However, the assignee is not obligated for liabilities which are unknown to the assignee at the time the assignee became a member and which could not be ascertained from the articles of organization or the operating agreement.

(3)   If an assignee of a limited liability company interest becomes a member, the assignor is not released from liability to the limited liability company under ss. 608.4211, 608.4228, and 608.426.

(4)   On application to a court of competent jurisdiction by any judgment creditor of a member, the court may charge the limited liability company membership interest of the member with payment of the unsatisfied amount of the judgment with interest. To the extent so charged, the judgment creditor has only the rights of an assignee of such interest. This chapter does not deprive any member of the benefit of any exemption laws applicable to the member's interest.

History.—

s. 34, ch. 93-284; s. 56, ch. 97-102; s. 1, ch. 99-315.

608.434   Power of estate of deceased or incompetent member; dissolved or terminated member.—

(1)   If a member who is an individual dies or if a court of competent jurisdiction adjudges a member who is an individual to be incompetent to manage the member's person or property, the member's executor, administrator, guardian, conservator, or other legal representative may exercise all the member's rights for the purpose of settling the member's estate or administering the member's property, including any power the member had to give an assignee the right to become a member.

(2)   If a member is a corporation, limited liability company, trust, or other entity and is dissolved or terminated, the powers of that member may be exercised by its legal representative or successor.

History.—

s. 35, ch. 93-284; s. 57, ch. 97-102; s. 1, ch. 99-315.

608.4351   Appraisal rights; definitions.—

The following definitions apply to this section and ss. 608.4352-608.43595:

(1)   "Affiliate" means a person that directly or indirectly, through one or more intermediaries, controls, is controlled by, or is under common control with another person. For purposes of s. 608.4352(2)(d), a person is deemed to be an affiliate of its senior executives.

(2)   "Appraisal event" means an event described in s. 608.4352(1).

(3)   "Beneficial member" means a person who is the beneficial owner of a membership interest held in a voting trust or by a nominee on the beneficial owner's behalf.

(4)   "Converted entity" means the other business entity into which a domestic limited liability company converts pursuant to ss. 608.4401-608.4404.

(5)   "Fair value" means the value of the member's membership interests determined:

(a)   Immediately before the effectuation of the appraisal event to which the member objects.

(b)   Using customary and current valuation concepts and techniques generally employed for similar businesses in the context of the transaction requiring appraisal, excluding any appreciation or depreciation in anticipation of the transaction to which the member objects unless exclusion would be inequitable to the limited liability company and its remaining members.

(c)   For a limited liability company with 10 or fewer members, without discounting for lack of marketability or minority status.

(6)   "Interest" means interest from the effective date of the appraisal event to which the member objects until the date of payment, at the rate of interest determined for judgments in accordance with s. 55.03, determined as of the effective date of the appraisal event.

(7)   "Limited liability company" means the domestic limited liability company that issued the membership interest held by a member demanding appraisal and, for matters covered in ss. 608.4352-608.43595, includes the converted entity in a conversion or the surviving entity in a merger.

(8)   "Record member" means each person who is identified as a member in the current list of members maintained in accordance with s. 608.4101 by the limited liability company, or to the extent the limited liability company has failed to

maintain a current list, each person that is the rightful owner of a membership interest in the limited liability company. An assignee of a membership interest is not a record member.

(9) "Senior executive" means a manager or managing member or the chief executive officer, chief operating officer, chief financial officer, or anyone in charge of a principal business unit or function of a limited liability company or of a manager or managing member of the limited liability company.

(10) "Member" means a record member or a beneficial member.

(11) "Membership interest" has the same meaning set forth in s. 608.402, except, if the appraisal rights of a member under s. 608.4352 pertain to only a certain class or series of a membership interest, the term "membership interest" means only the membership interest pertaining to such class or series.

(12) "Surviving entity" means the other business entity into which a domestic limited liability company is merged pursuant to ss. 608.438-608.4383.

History.—

s. 6, ch. 2005-267.

608.4352 Right of members to appraisal.—

(1) A member of a domestic limited liability company is entitled to appraisal rights, and to obtain payment of the fair value of that member's membership interest, in the following events:

(a) Consummation of a merger of such limited liability company pursuant to this act and the member possessed the right to vote upon the merger; or

(b) Consummation of a conversion of such limited liability company pursuant to this act and the member possessed the right to vote upon the conversion.

(2) Notwithstanding subsection (1), the availability of appraisal rights shall be limited in accordance with the following provisions:

(a) Appraisal rights shall not be available for membership interests which are:

1. Listed on the New York Stock Exchange or the American Stock Exchange or designated as a national market system security on an interdealer quotation system by the National Association of Securities Dealers, Inc.; or

2. Not listed or designated as provided in subparagraph 1. but are issued by a limited liability company that has at least 500 members and all membership interests of the limited liability company, including membership interests that are limited to a right to receive distributions, have a market value of at least $10 million, exclusive of the value of any such interests held by its managing members, managers, and other senior executives owning more than 10 percent of the rights to receive distributions from the limited liability company.

(b) The applicability of paragraph (a) shall be determined as of the date fixed to determine the members entitled to receive notice of, and to vote upon, the appraisal event.

(c) Paragraph (a) shall not apply, and appraisal rights shall be available pursuant to subsection (1), for any members who are required by the appraisal event to accept for their membership interests anything other than cash or a proprietary interest of an entity that satisfies the standards set forth in paragraph (a) at the time the appraisal event becomes effective.

(d) Paragraph (a) shall not apply, and appraisal rights shall be available pursuant to subsection (1), for the holders of a membership interest if:

1. Any of the members' interests in the limited liability company or the limited liability company's assets are being acquired or converted, whether by merger, conversion, or otherwise, pursuant to the appraisal event by a person, or by an affiliate of a person, who:

a. Is, or at any time in the 1-year period immediately preceding approval of the appraisal event was, the beneficial owner of 20 percent or more of those interests in the limited liability company entitled to vote on the appraisal event, excluding any such interests acquired pursuant to an offer for all interests having such voting rights if such offer was made within 1 year prior to the appraisal event for consideration of the same kind and of a value equal to or less than that paid in connection with the appraisal event; or

b. Directly or indirectly has, or at any time in the 1-year period immediately preceding approval of the appraisal event had, the power, contractually or otherwise, to cause the appointment or election of any senior executives; or

2. Any of the members' interests in the limited liability company or the limited liability company's assets are being acquired or converted, whether by merger, conversion, or otherwise, pursuant to the appraisal event by a person, or by an affiliate of a person, who is, or at any time in the 1-year period immediately preceding approval of the appraisal event was, a senior executive of the limited liability company or a senior executive of any affiliate of the limited liability company, and that senior executive will receive, as a result of the limited liability company action, a financial benefit not generally available to members, other than:

a. Employment, consulting, retirement, or similar benefits established separately and not as part of or in contemplation of the appraisal event;

b. Employment, consulting, retirement, or similar benefits established in contemplation of, or as part of, the appraisal event that are not more favorable than those existing before the appraisal event or, if more favorable, that have been approved by the limited liability company; or

c. In the case of a managing member or manager of the limited liability company who will, during or as the result of the appraisal event, become a managing member, manager, general partner, or director of the surviving or converted entity or one of its affiliates, those rights and benefits as a managing member, manager, general partner, or director that are provided on the same basis as those afforded by the surviving or converted entity generally to other managing members, managers, general partners, or directors of the surviving or converted entity or its affiliate.

(e) For the purposes of sub-subparagraph (d)1.a. only, the term "beneficial owner" means any person who, directly or indirectly, through any contract, arrangement, or understanding, other than a revocable proxy, has or shares the right to vote, or to direct the voting of, an interest in a limited liability company with respect to approval of the appraisal event, provided a member of a national securities exchange shall not be deemed to be a beneficial owner of an interest in a limited liability company held directly or indirectly by it on behalf of another person solely because such member is the record-holder of interests in the limited liability company if the member is precluded by the rules of such exchange from voting without instruction on contested matters or matters that may affect substantially the rights or privileges of the holders of the interests in the limited liability company to be voted. When two or more persons agree to act together for the purpose of voting such interests, each member of the group formed thereby shall be deemed to have acquired beneficial ownership, as of the date of such agreement, of all voting interests in the limited liability company beneficially owned by any member of the group.

(3) A member entitled to appraisal rights under this section and ss. 608.4353-608.43595 may not challenge a completed appraisal event unless the appraisal event:

(a) Was not effectuated in accordance with the applicable provisions of this section and ss. 608.4353-608.43595, or the limited liability company's articles of organization or operating agreement; or

(b)   Was procured as a result of fraud or material misrepresentation.

(4)   A limited liability company may modify, restrict, or eliminate the appraisal rights provided in this section and ss. 608.4353-608.43595 in its operating agreement.

History.—
s. 6, ch. 2005-267.

608.4353   Assertion of rights by nominees and beneficial owners.—

(1)   A record member may assert appraisal rights as to fewer than all the membership interests registered in the record member's name which are owned by a beneficial member only if the record member objects with respect to all membership interests of the class or series owned by that beneficial member and notifies the limited liability company in writing of the name and address of each beneficial member on whose behalf appraisal rights are being asserted. The rights of a record member who asserts appraisal rights for only part of the membership interests of the class or series held of record in the record member's name under this subsection shall be determined as if the membership interests to which the record member objects and the record member's other membership interests were registered in the names of different record members.

(2)   A beneficial member may assert appraisal rights as to a membership interest held on behalf of the member only if such beneficial member:

(a)   Submits to the limited liability company the record member's written consent to the assertion of such rights no later than the date referred to in s. 608.4356(2)(b)2.

(b)   Does so with respect to all membership interests of the class or series that are beneficially owned by the beneficial member.

History.—
s. 6, ch. 2005-267.

608.4354   Notice of appraisal rights.—

(1)   If a proposed appraisal event is to be submitted to a vote at a members' meeting, the meeting notice must state that the limited liability company has concluded that members are, are not, or may be entitled to assert appraisal rights under this act.

(2)   If the limited liability company concludes that appraisal rights are or may be available, a copy of ss. 608.4351-608.43595 must accompany the meeting notice sent to those record members entitled to exercise appraisal rights.

(3)   If the appraisal event is to be approved other than by a members' meeting, the notice referred to in subsection (1) must be sent to all members at the time that consents are first solicited, whether or not consents are solicited from all members, and include the materials described in s. 608.4356.

History.—
s. 6, ch. 2005-267.

608.4355   Notice of intent to demand payment.—

(1)   If a proposed appraisal event is submitted to a vote at a members' meeting, or is submitted to a member pursuant to a consent vote, a member who is entitled to and who wishes to assert appraisal rights with respect to any class or series of membership interests:

(a)   Must deliver to a manager or managing member of the limited liability company before the vote is taken, or within 20 days after receiving the notice pursuant to s. 608.4354(3) if action is to be taken without a member meeting, written notice of such person's intent to demand payment if the proposed appraisal event is effectuated.

(b)   Must not vote, or cause or permit to be voted, any membership interests of such class or series in favor of the appraisal event.

(2)   A person who may otherwise be entitled to appraisal rights, but who does not satisfy the requirements of subsection (1), is not entitled to payment under ss. 608.4351-608.43595.

History.—
s. 6, ch. 2005-267; s. 69, ch. 2006-1.

608.4356   Appraisal notice and form.—

(1)   If the proposed appraisal event becomes effective, the limited liability company must deliver a written appraisal notice and form required by paragraph (2)(a) to all members who satisfied the requirements of s. 608.4355.

(2)   The appraisal notice must be sent no earlier than the date the appraisal event became effective and no later than 10 days after such date and must:

(a)   Supply a form that specifies the date that the appraisal event became effective and that provides for the member to state:

1.   The member's name and address.

2.   The number, classes, and series of membership interests as to which the member asserts appraisal rights.

3.   That the member did not vote for the transaction.

4.   Whether the member accepts the limited liability company's offer as stated in subparagraph (b)4.

5.   If the offer is not accepted, the member's estimated fair value of the membership interests and a demand for payment of the member's estimated value plus interest.

(b)   State:

1.   Where the form described in paragraph (a) must be sent.

2.   A date by which the limited liability company must receive the form, which date may not be fewer than 40 nor more than 60 days after the date the appraisal notice and form described in this subsection are sent, and that the member shall have waived the right to demand appraisal with respect to the membership interests unless the form is received by the limited liability company by such specified date.

3.   In the case of membership interests represented by a certificate, the location at which certificates for such certificated membership interests must be deposited, if that action is required by the limited liability company, and the date by which those certificates must be deposited, which date may not be earlier than the date for receiving the required form under subparagraph 2.

4.   The limited liability company's estimate of the fair value of the membership interests.

5.   An offer to each member who is entitled to appraisal rights to pay the limited liability company's estimate of fair value set forth in subparagraph 4.

6.   That, if requested in writing, the limited liability company will provide to the member so requesting, within 10 days after the date specified in subparagraph 2., the number of members who return the forms by the specified date and the total number of membership interests owned by them.

7.   The date by which the notice to withdraw under s. 608.4357 must be received, which date must be within 20 days after the date specified in subparagraph 2.

(c)   Be accompanied by:

1.   Financial statements of the limited liability company that issued the membership interests to be appraised, consisting of a balance sheet as of the end of the fiscal year ending not more than 15 months prior to the date of the limited liability company's appraisal notice, an income statement for that year, a cash flow statement for that year, and the latest available interim financial statements, if any.

2.   A copy of ss. 608.4351-608.43595.

History.—
s. 6, ch. 2005-267.

608.4357   Perfection of rights; right to withdraw.—

(1)   A member who wishes to exercise appraisal rights must execute and return the form received pursuant to s. 608.4356(1) and, in the case of certificated membership interests and if the limited liability company so requires, deposit the member's certificates in accordance with the terms of the

notice by the date referred to in the notice pursuant to s. 608.4356(2)(b)2. Once a member deposits that member's certificates or, in the case of uncertificated membership interests, returns the executed form described in s. 608.4356(2), the member loses all rights as a member, unless the member withdraws pursuant to subsection (3). Upon receiving a demand for payment from a member who holds an uncertificated membership interest, the limited liability company shall make an appropriate notation of the demand for payment in its records.

(2)   The limited liability company may restrict the transfer of such membership interests from the date the member delivers the items required by subsection (1).

(3)   A member who has complied with subsection (1) may nevertheless decline to exercise appraisal rights and withdraw from the appraisal process by so notifying the limited liability company in writing by the date set forth in the appraisal notice pursuant to s. 608.4356(2)(b)7. A member who fails to so withdraw from the appraisal process may not thereafter withdraw without the limited liability company's written consent.

(4)   A member who does not execute and return the form and, in the case of certificated membership interests, deposit that member's certificates, if so required by the limited liability company, each by the date set forth in the notice described in subsection (2), shall not be entitled to payment under this chapter.

(5)   If the member's right to receive fair value is terminated other than by the purchase of the membership interest by the limited liability company, all rights of the member, with respect to such membership interest, shall be reinstated effective as of the date the member delivered the items required by subsection (1), including the right to receive any intervening payment or other distribution with respect to such membership interest, or, if any such rights have expired or any such distribution other than a cash payment has been completed, in lieu thereof at the election of the limited liability company, the fair value thereof in cash as determined by the limited liability company as of the time of such expiration or completion, but without prejudice otherwise to any action or proceeding of the limited liability company that may have been taken by the limited liability company on or after the date the member delivered the items required by subsection (1).

History.—
s. 6, ch. 2005-267.

608.43575 Member's acceptance of limited liability company's offer.—

(1)   If the member states on the form provided in s. 608.4356(1) that the member accepts the offer of the limited liability company to pay the limited liability company's estimated fair value for the membership interest, the limited liability company shall make such payment to the member within 90 days after the limited liability company's receipt of the items required by s. 608.4357(1).

(2)   Upon payment of the agreed value, the member shall cease to have any interest in the membership interest.

History.—
s. 6, ch. 2005-267.

608.4358   Procedure if member is dissatisfied with offer.—

(1)   A member who is dissatisfied with the limited liability company's offer as set forth pursuant to s. 608.4356(2)(b)5. must notify the limited liability company on the form provided pursuant to s. 608.4356(1) of the member's estimate of the fair value of the membership interest and demand payment of that estimate plus interest.

(2)   A member who fails to notify the limited liability company in writing of the member's demand to be paid the member's estimate of the fair value plus interest under subsection (1) within the timeframe set forth in s.

608.4356(2)(b)2. waives the right to demand payment under this section and shall be entitled only to the payment offered by the limited liability company pursuant to s. 608.4356(2)(b)5.

History.—
s. 6, ch. 2005-267.

608.43585   Court action.—

(1)   If a member makes demand for payment under s. 608.4358 which remains unsettled, the limited liability company shall commence a proceeding within 60 days after receiving the payment demand and petition the court to determine the fair value of the membership interest and accrued interest. If the limited liability company does not commence the proceeding within the 60-day period, any member who has made a demand pursuant to s. 608.4358 may commence the proceeding in the name of the limited liability company.

(2)   The proceeding shall be commenced in the appropriate court of the county in which the limited liability company's principal office in this state is located or, if none, the county in which its registered agent is located. If the limited liability company is a foreign limited liability company without a registered agent in this state, the proceeding shall be commenced in the county in this state in which the principal office or registered agent of the domestic limited liability company was located at the time of the appraisal event.

(3)   All members, whether or not residents of this state, whose demands remain unsettled shall be made parties to the proceeding as in an action against their membership interests. The limited liability company shall serve a copy of the initial pleading in such proceeding upon each member party who is a resident of this state in the manner provided by law for the service of a summons and complaint and upon each nonresident member party by registered or certified mail or by publication as provided by law.

(4)   The jurisdiction of the court in which the proceeding is commenced under subsection (2) is plenary and exclusive. If it so elects, the court may appoint one or more persons as appraisers to receive evidence and recommend a decision on the question of fair value. The appraisers shall have the powers described in the order appointing them or in any amendment to the order. The members demanding appraisal rights are entitled to the same discovery rights as parties in other civil proceedings. There shall be no right to a jury trial.

(5)   Each member made a party to the proceeding is entitled to judgment for the amount of the fair value of such member's membership interests, plus interest, as found by the court.

(6)   The limited liability company shall pay each such member the amount found to be due within 10 days after final determination of the proceedings. Upon payment of the judgment, the member shall cease to have any interest in the membership interests.

History.—
s. 6, ch. 2005-267.

608.4359   Court costs and counsel fees.—

(1)   The court in an appraisal proceeding shall determine all costs of the proceeding, including the reasonable compensation and expenses of appraisers appointed by the court. The court shall assess the costs against the limited liability company, except that the court may assess costs against all or some of the members demanding appraisal, in amounts the court finds equitable, to the extent the court finds such members acted arbitrarily, vexatiously, or not in good faith with respect to the rights provided by this chapter.

(2)   The court in an appraisal proceeding may also assess the fees and expenses of counsel and experts for the respective parties, in amounts the court finds equitable:

(a)   Against the limited liability company and in favor of any or all members demanding appraisal if the court finds the limited liability company did not substantially comply with ss. 608.4353 and 608.4356; or

(b)   Against either the limited liability company or a member demanding appraisal, in favor of any other party, if the court finds that the party against whom the fees and expenses are assessed acted arbitrarily, vexatiously, or not in good faith with respect to the rights provided by this chapter.

(3)   If the court in an appraisal proceeding finds that the services of counsel for any member were of substantial benefit to other members similarly situated, and that the fees for those services should not be assessed against the limited liability company, the court may award to such counsel reasonable fees to be paid out of the amounts awarded the members who were benefited.

(4)   To the extent the limited liability company fails to make a required payment pursuant to s. 608.43575, the member may sue directly for the amount owed and, to the extent successful, shall be entitled to recover from the limited liability company all costs and expenses of the suit, including attorney's fees.

History.—
s. 6, ch. 2005-267.

608.43595   Limitation on limited liability company payment.—
(1)   No payment shall be made to a member seeking appraisal rights if, at the time of payment, the limited liability company is unable to meet the distribution standards of s. 608.428. In such event, the member shall, at the member's option:

(a)   Withdraw the notice of intent to assert appraisal rights, which shall in such event be deemed withdrawn with the consent of the limited liability company; or

(b)   Retain the status as a claimant against the limited liability company and, if the limited liability company is liquidated, be subordinated to the rights of creditors of the limited liability company but have rights superior to the members not asserting appraisal rights and, if it is not liquidated, retain the right to be paid for the membership interest, which right the limited liability company shall be obliged to satisfy when the restrictions of this section do not apply.

(2)   The member shall exercise the option under paragraph (1)(a) or paragraph (1)(b) by written notice filed with the limited liability company within 30 days after the limited liability company has given written notice that the payment for the membership interests cannot be made because of the restrictions of this section. If the member fails to exercise the option, the member shall be deemed to have withdrawn the notice of intent to assert appraisal rights.

History.—
s. 6, ch. 2005-267.

608.438   Merger of limited liability company.—
(1)   As used in this section and ss. 608.4381-608.4383, the term "other business entity" or "another business entity" means a corporation, a limited liability company, a common law or business trust or association, a real estate investment trust, a general partnership, including a limited liability partnership, a limited partnership, including a limited liability limited partnership, or any other domestic or foreign entity that is organized under a governing law or other applicable law.

(2)   Unless otherwise provided in the articles of organization or the operating agreement of a limited liability company, pursuant to a plan of merger, a limited liability company may merge with or into one or more limited liability companies or other business entities formed, organized, or incorporated under the laws of this state or any other state, the United States, foreign country, or other foreign jurisdiction, if:

(a)   Each limited liability company that is a party to the merger complies with the applicable provisions of this chapter and complies with the terms of its articles of organization and operating agreement.

(b)   Each domestic partnership that is a party to the merger complies with the applicable provisions of chapter 620.

(c)   Each domestic corporation that is a party to the merger complies with the applicable provisions of chapter 607.

(d)   The merger is permitted by the laws of the state, country, or jurisdiction under which each other business entity that is a party to the merger is formed, organized, or incorporated, and each such other business entity complies with such laws in effecting the merger.

(3)   The plan of merger shall set forth:
(a)   The name of each limited liability company and the name and jurisdiction of formation, organization, or incorporation of each other business entity planning to merge, and the name of the surviving or resulting limited liability company or other business entity into which each other limited liability company or other business entity plans to merge, which is, in this section and in ss. 608.4381-608.4383, designated as the surviving entity.

(b)   The terms and conditions of the merger.

(c)   The manner and basis of converting the interests of the members of each limited liability company that is a party to the merger and the interests, partnership interests, shares, obligations, or other securities of each other business entity that is a party to the merger into interests, partnership interests, shares, obligations, or other securities of the surviving entity or any other limited liability company or other business entity or, in whole or in part, into cash or other property, and the manner and basis of converting rights to acquire interests of each limited liability company that is a party to the merger and rights to acquire interests, partnership interests, shares, obligations, or other securities of each other business entity that is a party to the merger into rights to acquire interests, partnership interests, shares, obligations, or other securities of the surviving entity or any other limited liability company or other business entity or, in whole or in part, into cash or other property.

(d)   All statements required to be set forth in the plan of merger by the laws under which each other business entity that is a party to the merger is formed, organized, or incorporated.

(4)   The plan of merger may set forth:
(a)   If a limited liability company is to be the surviving entity, any amendments to, or a restatement of, the articles of organization or the operating agreement of the surviving entity, and such amendments or restatement shall be effective at the effective date of the merger.

(b)   The effective date of the merger, which may be on or after the date of filing the certificate of merger.

(c)   A provision authorizing one or more of the limited liability companies that are parties to the merger to abandon the proposed merger pursuant to s. 608.4381(7).

(d)   A statement of, or a statement of the method of determining, the "fair value," as defined in s. 608.4351, of an interest in any domestic limited liability company that is a party to the merger.

(e)   Other provisions relating to the merger.

History.—
s. 5, ch. 98-101; s. 1, ch. 99-315; s. 23, ch. 2002-272; s. 7, ch. 2005-267.

608.4381   Action on plan of merger.—
(1)   Unless the articles of organization or the operating agreement of a limited liability company require a greater than majority vote, the plan of merger shall be approved in writing by a majority of the managers who are members of a limited liability company that is a party to the merger in which management is not reserved to its members. If no manager is a member, the plan of merger shall be approved by vote of the members as set forth in this section. Unless the

articles of organization or the operating agreement of a limited liability company require a greater than majority vote or provide for another method of determining the voting rights of each of its members, and whether or not management is reserved to its members, the plan of merger shall be approved in writing by a majority-in-interest of the members of a limited liability company that is a party to the merger, and, if applicable, the vote of each member shall be weighted in accordance with s. 608.4231; provided, unless the articles of organization or the operating agreement of the limited liability company require a greater than majority vote or provide for another method of determining the voting rights of each of its members, if there is more than one class or group of members, the merger shall be approved by a majority-in-interest of the members of each such class or group, and, if applicable, the vote of each member shall be weighted in accordance with s. 608.4231.

(2) In addition to the approval required by subsection (1), if the surviving entity is a partnership or limited partnership, no member of a limited liability company that is a party to the merger shall, as a result of the merger, become a general partner of such partnership or limited partnership unless such member specifically consents in writing to becoming a general partner of such partnership or limited partnership, and unless such written consent is obtained from each such member, such merger shall not become effective under s. 608.4383. Any member providing such consent in writing shall be deemed to have voted in favor of the plan of merger for purposes of ss. 608.4351-608.43595.

(3) All members of each limited liability company that is a party to the merger shall be given written notice of any meeting or other action with respect to the approval of a plan of merger as provided in subsection (4), not fewer than 30 or more than 60 days before the date of the meeting at which the plan of merger shall be submitted for approval by the members of such limited liability company; provided, if the plan of merger is submitted to the members of the limited liability company for their written approval or other action without a meeting, such notification shall be given to each member not fewer than 30 or more than 60 days before the effective date of the merger. Pursuant to s. 608.455, the notification required by this subsection may be waived in writing by the person or persons entitled to such notification.

(4) The notification required by subsection (3) shall be in writing and shall include:

(a) The date, time, and place of the meeting, if any, at which the plan of merger is to be submitted for approval by the members of the limited liability company, or, if the plan of merger is to be submitted for written approval or by other action without a meeting, a statement to that effect.

(b) A copy or summary of the plan of merger.

(c) The statement or statements required by ss. 608.4351-608.43595 regarding availability of appraisal rights, if any, to members of the limited liability company.

(d) The date on which such notification was mailed or delivered to the members.

(e) Any other information concerning the plan of merger.

(5) The notification required by subsection (3) shall be deemed to be given at the earliest date of:

(a) The date such notification is received;

(b) Five days after the date such notification is deposited in the United States mail addressed to the member at the member's address as it appears in the books and records of the limited liability company, with postage thereon prepaid;

(c) The date shown on the return receipt, if sent by registered or certified mail, return receipt requested, and the receipt is signed by or on behalf of the addressee; or

(d) The date such notification is given in accordance with the provisions of the articles of organization or the operating agreement of the limited liability company.

(6) A plan of merger may provide for the manner, if any, in which the plan of merger may be amended at any time before the effective date of the merger, except after the approval of the plan of merger by the members of a limited liability company that is a party to the merger, the plan of merger may not be amended to:

(a) Change the amount or kind of interests, partnership interests, shares, obligations, other securities, cash, rights, or any other property to be received by the members of such limited liability company in exchange for or on conversion of their interests;

(b) If the surviving entity is a limited liability company, change any term of the articles of organization or the operating agreement of the surviving entity, except for changes that otherwise could be adopted without the approval of the members of the surviving entity;

(c) If the surviving entity is not a limited liability company, change any term of the articles of incorporation or comparable governing document of the surviving entity, except for changes that otherwise could be adopted by the board of directors or comparable representatives of the surviving entity; or

(d) Change any of the terms and conditions of the plan of merger if any such change, alone or in the aggregate, would materially and adversely affect the members, or any class or group of members, of such limited liability company.

If an amendment to a plan of merger is made in accordance with the plan and articles of merger have been filed with the Department of State, an amended certificate of merger executed by each limited liability company and other business entity that is a party to the merger shall be filed with the Department of State prior to the effective date of the merger.

(7) Unless the limited liability company's articles of organization or operating agreement or the plan of merger provide otherwise, notwithstanding the prior approval of the plan of merger by any limited liability company that is a party to the merger in which management is not reserved to its members, and at any time prior to the filing of articles of merger with the Department of State, the planned merger may be abandoned, subject to any contractual rights, by any such limited liability company by the affirmative vote of a majority of its managers without further action by its members, in accordance with the procedure set forth in the plan of merger or, if none is set forth, in the manner determined by the managers of such limited liability company.

History.—
s. 5, ch. 98-101; s. 33, ch. 99-7; s. 1, ch. 99-315; s. 8, ch. 2005-267; s. 70, ch. 2006-1.

608.4382 Certificate of merger.—

(1) After a plan of merger is approved by each limited liability company and each other business entity that is a party to the merger, the surviving entity shall deliver to the Department of State for filing a certificate of merger, which shall be executed by each limited liability company and by each other business entity as required by applicable law, and which shall set forth:

(a) The plan of merger.

(b) A statement that the plan of merger was approved by each limited liability company that is a party to the merger in accordance with the applicable provisions of this chapter, and, if applicable, a statement that the written consent of each member of such limited liability company who, as a result of the merger, becomes a general partner of the surviving entity has been obtained pursuant to s. 608.4381(2).

(c)   A statement that the plan of merger was approved by each domestic partnership that is a party to the merger in accordance with the applicable provisions of chapter 620.

(d)   A statement that the plan of merger was approved by each domestic corporation that is a party to the merger in accordance with the applicable provisions of chapter 607.

(e)   A statement that the plan of merger was approved by each other business entity that is a party to the merger, other than limited liability companies, partnerships, and corporations formed, organized, or incorporated under the laws of this state, in accordance with the applicable laws of the state, country, or jurisdiction under which such other business entity is formed, organized, or incorporated.

(f)   The effective date of the merger, which may be on or after the date of filing the certificate of merger, subject to the limitations in s. 608.409(2), provided, if the certificate of merger does not provide for an effective date of the merger, the effective date shall be the date on which the certificate of merger is filed.

(g)   If the surviving entity is another business entity formed, organized, or incorporated under the laws of any state, country, or jurisdiction other than this state:

1.   The address, including street and number, if any, of its principal office under the laws of the state, country, or jurisdiction in which it was formed, organized, or incorporated.

2.   If the surviving entity is a foreign entity and is not authorized to transact business in this state, a statement that the surviving entity appoints the Secretary of State as its agent for service of process in a proceeding to enforce obligations of each limited liability company that merged into such entity, including any appraisal rights of its members under ss. 608.4351-608.43595, and the street and mailing address of an office which the Department of State may use for purposes of s. 48.181.

3.   A statement that the surviving entity has agreed to pay to any members with appraisal rights the amount to which such members are entitled under ss. 608.4351-608.43595.

(2)   A copy of the certificate of merger, certified by the Department of State, may be filed in the official records of any county in this state in which any party to the merger holds an interest in real property.

History.—

s. 5, ch. 98-101; s. 9, ch. 2005-267.

608.4383   Effect of merger.—

When a merger becomes effective:

(1)   Every limited liability company and other business entity that is a party to the merger merges into the surviving entity and the separate existence of every limited liability company and other business entity that is a party to the merger, except the surviving entity, ceases.

(2)   The title to all real estate and other property, or any interest therein, owned by each domestic limited liability company and other business entity that is a party to the merger is vested in the surviving entity without reversion or impairment by reason of this chapter.

(3)   The surviving entity shall thereafter be responsible and liable for all the liabilities and obligations of each limited liability company and other business entity that is a party to the merger, including liabilities arising out of the appraisal rights under ss. 608.4351-608.43595 with respect to such merger under applicable law.

(4)   Any claim existing or action or proceeding pending by or against any limited liability company or other business entity that is a party to the merger may be continued as if the merger did not occur or the surviving entity may be substituted in the proceeding for the limited liability company or other business entity which ceased existence.

(5)   Neither the rights of creditors nor any liens upon the property of any limited liability company or other business entity shall be impaired by such merger.

(6)   If a limited liability company is the surviving entity, the articles of organization and the operating agreement of such limited liability company in effect immediately prior to the time the merger becomes effective shall be the articles of organization and the operating agreement of the surviving entity, except as amended or restated to the extent provided in the plan of merger.

(7)   The partnership and membership interests, shares, obligations, or other securities and other interests, and the rights to acquire such shares, obligations, or other securities and other interests, of each limited liability company and other business entity that is a party to the merger shall be converted into partnership and membership interests, shares, obligations, or other securities and other interests, or rights to such securities, obligations, or other interests, of the surviving entity or, in whole or in part, into cash or other property as provided in the plan of merger, and the former members of each limited liability company merging into another business entity shall be entitled only to the rights provided in the plan of merger and to their appraisal rights, if any, under ss. 608.4351-608.43595, or other applicable law.

History.—

s. 5, ch. 98-101; s. 1, ch. 99-315; s. 3, ch. 2000-298; s. 10, ch. 2005-267.

608.439   Conversion of certain entities to a limited liability company.—

(1)   As used in this section, the term "other business entity" or "another business entity" means a common law or business trust or association; a real estate investment trust; a general partnership, including a limited liability partnership; a limited partnership, including a limited liability limited partnership; or any other domestic or foreign entity that is organized under a governing law or other applicable law, provided such term shall not include a domestic limited liability company.

(2)   Any other business entity may convert to a domestic limited liability company if the conversion is permitted by the laws of the jurisdiction that enacted the statute or other applicable law governing the other business entity and the other business entity complies with such laws and the requirements of this section in effecting the conversion. The other business entity shall file with the Department of State in accordance with s. 608.4081:

(a)   A certificate of conversion that has been executed by one or more authorized persons in accordance with s. 608.408.

(b)   Articles of organization that comply with s. 608.407 and have been executed by one or more authorized persons in accordance with s. 608.408.

(3)   The certificate of conversion to a limited liability company shall state:

(a)   The date on which and jurisdiction in which the other entity was first organized and, if it has changed, its jurisdiction immediately prior to its conversion to a domestic limited liability company.

(b)   The name of the other entity immediately prior to the filing of the certificate of conversion.

(c)   The name of the limited liability company as set forth in its articles of organization filed in accordance with subsection (2).

(d)   Subject to the limitations in s. 608.409(2), the delayed effective date or time (which shall be a date or time certain) of the conversion to a limited liability company if it is not to be effective upon the filing of the certificate of conversion and the articles of organization, provided such delayed effective date and time may not be different than the effective date of the articles of organization.

(4)   Upon the filing in the Department of State of the certificate of conversion to a limited liability company and the articles of organization or upon the delayed effective date or time of the certificate of conversion and the articles of organization, the other entity shall be converted into a domestic limited liability company and the limited liability company shall thereafter be subject to all of the provisions of this chapter, except that notwithstanding s. 608.409, the existence of the limited liability company shall be deemed to have commenced when the other entity commenced its existence in the jurisdiction in which the other entity was first organized.

(5)   The conversion of any other entity into a domestic limited liability company shall not affect any obligations or liabilities of the other entity incurred prior to its conversion into a domestic limited liability company or the personal liability of any person incurred prior to such conversion.

(6)   When any conversion becomes effective under this section, for all purposes of the laws of this state, all of the rights, privileges, and powers of the other entity that has converted, and all property, real, personal, and mixed, and all debts due to such other entity, as well as all other things and causes of action belonging to such other entity, shall be vested in the domestic limited liability company into which it was converted and shall thereafter be the property of the domestic limited liability company as they were of the other entity that has converted, and the title to any real property vested by deed or otherwise in such other entity shall not revert or be in any way impaired by reason of this chapter, but all rights of creditors and all liens upon any property of such other entity shall be preserved unimpaired, and all debts, liabilities, and duties of the other entity that has converted shall thenceforth attach to the domestic limited liability company and may be enforced against it to the same extent as if said debts, liabilities, and duties had been incurred or contracted by it.

(7)   Unless otherwise agreed, or as required under applicable non-Florida law, the converting entity shall not be required to wind up its affairs or pay its liabilities and distribute its assets, and the conversion shall not constitute a dissolution of the converting entity and shall constitute a continuation of the existence of the converting entity in the form of a domestic limited liability company.

(8)   Prior to filing a certificate of conversion with the Department of State, the conversion shall be approved in the manner provided for by the document, instrument, agreement, or other writing, as the case may be, governing the internal affairs of the other entity and the conduct of its business or by applicable law, as appropriate, and the articles of organization or operating agreement shall be approved by the same authorization required to approve the conversion. As part of such an approval, a plan of conversion or other record may describe the manner and basis of converting the shares, partnership interests, limited liability company interests, obligations, or securities of, or other interests in, the other business entity which is to be converted, or any rights to acquire any such shares, interests, obligations, or other securities, into limited liability company interests, obligations, or other securities of the domestic limited liability company, or rights to acquire interests, obligations, or other securities or, in whole or in part, into cash or other consideration. Such a plan or other record may also contain other provisions relating to the conversion, including without limitation the right of the other business entity to abandon a proposed conversion, or an effective date for the conversion that is not inconsistent with paragraph (3)(d).

(9)   The provisions of this section shall not be construed to limit the accomplishment of a change in the law governing, or the domicile of, any other entity to this state by any other means provided for in the articles of organization or operating agreement or other agreement or as otherwise permitted by law, including by the amendment of the articles of organization or operating agreement or other agreement.

History.—

s. 1, ch. 99-315; s. 11, ch. 2005-267.

608.4401   Conversion of a domestic limited liability company into another business entity.—

(1)   As used in this section and ss. 608.4402, 608.4403, and 608.4404, the term "other business entity" or "another business entity" means a corporation; a common law or business trust or association; a real estate investment trust; a general partnership, including a limited liability partnership; a limited partnership, including a limited liability limited partnership; or any other domestic or foreign entity that is organized under a governing law or other applicable law, provided such term shall not include a domestic limited liability company.

(2)   Pursuant to a plan of conversion complying and approved in accordance with this section and s. 608.4402, a domestic limited liability company may convert to another business entity organized under the laws of this state or any other state, the United States, a foreign country, or any other foreign jurisdiction, if:

(a)   The domestic limited liability company converting to the other business entity complies with the applicable provisions of this chapter and any applicable terms in its articles of organization and operating agreement.

(b)   The conversion is permitted by the laws of the jurisdiction that enacted the law or other applicable law under which the other business entity is governed and the other business entity complies with such laws in effecting the conversion.

(3)   The plan of conversion shall set forth:

(a)   The name of the domestic limited liability company and the name and jurisdiction of the other business entity into which the domestic limited liability company is to be converted.

(b)   The terms and conditions of the conversion, including the manner and basis of converting the limited liability company interests or other securities, or any rights to acquire limited liability company interests or other securities, of the domestic limited liability company into the partnership interests, shares, obligations, securities, or other interests in the other business entity, or any rights to acquire any partnership interests, shares, obligations, securities, or other interests, or, in whole or in part, into cash or other consideration.

(c)   The statements required to be set forth in the plan of conversion by the laws under which the other business entity is governed.

(4)   The plan of conversion shall include, or have attached, the articles, certificate, registration, or other organizational document by which the other business entity has been organized under its governing law.

(5)   A plan of conversion may provide for the manner, if any, in which the plan of conversion may be amended at any time before the effective date of the conversion, except after the approval of the plan of conversion by the members of the limited liability company to be converted, the plan of conversion may not be amended to:

(a)   Change the amount or kind of partnership interests, shares, obligations, securities, cash, rights, or any other consideration to be received by the members of such limited liability company in exchange for or on conversion of their member interests in or other securities of the limited liability company;

(b)   Change any term of the articles of incorporation or organization, bylaws, partnership or operating agreement, or comparable governing document of the surviving entity, except for changes that otherwise could be adopted without approval of the members approving the plan of conversion; or

(c)   Change any of the terms and conditions of the plan of

conversion if any such change, alone or in the aggregate, would materially and adversely affect the members, or any class or group of members, of such limited liability company. If an amendment to a plan of conversion is made in accordance with the plan of conversion and a certificate of conversion has been filed with the Department of State, an amended certificate of conversion executed by the limited liability company shall be filed with the Department of State prior to the effective date of the conversion.

(6)   The plan of conversion may also set forth any other provisions relating to the conversion, including, without limitation, a statement of the method of determining the fair value, as defined in s. 608.4351, of an interest in the limited liability company.

History.—
s. 12, ch. 2005-267.

608.4402   Action on plan of conversion.—
(1)   Unless the articles of organization or the operating agreement of a limited liability company requires a greater than majority vote, the plan of conversion shall be approved in writing by a majority of the managers who are members of a converting limited liability company in which management is not reserved to its members. If no manager is a member, the plan of conversion shall be approved by vote of the members as set forth in this section. Unless the articles of organization or the operating agreement of the converting limited liability company requires a greater than majority vote or provides for another method of determining the voting rights of each of its members, and whether or not management is reserved to its members, the plan of conversion shall be approved in writing by a majority-in-interest of the members of the converting limited liability company and, if applicable, the vote of each member shall be weighted in accordance with s. 608.4231, provided, unless the articles of organization or the operating agreement of the converting limited liability company requires a greater than majority vote or provides for another method of determining the voting rights of each of its members, if there is more than one class or group of members, the conversion shall be approved by a majority-in-interest of the members of each such class or group, and, if applicable, the vote of each member shall be weighted in accordance with s. 608.4231.

(2)   In addition to the approval required by subsection (1), if the other business entity is a partnership or limited partnership, no member of a converting limited liability company shall become a general partner of such partnership or limited partnership as a result of the conversion unless such member specifically consents in writing to becoming a general partner of such partnership or limited partnership, and, unless such written consent is obtained from each such member, the conversion shall not become effective under s. 608.4404. Any member providing such consent in writing shall also be deemed to have voted in favor of the plan of conversion for purposes of ss. 608.4351-608.43595.

(3)   All members of the limited liability company to be converted shall be given written notice of any meeting or other action with respect to the approval of a plan of conversion as provided in subsections (4) and (5), not fewer than 30 or more than 60 days before the date of the meeting at which the plan of conversion shall be submitted for approval by the members of such limited liability company, provided, if the plan of conversion is submitted to the members of the limited liability company for their written approval or other action without a meeting, such notification shall be given to each member not fewer than 30 or more than 60 days before the effective date of the conversion. Pursuant to s. 608.455, the notification required by this subsection may be waived in writing by any person entitled to such notification.

(4)   The notification required by subsection (3) shall be in writing and shall include:
(a)   The date, time, and place of the meeting, if any, at which the plan of conversion is to be submitted for approval by the members of the limited liability company or, if the plan of conversion is to be submitted for written approval or by other action without a meeting, a statement to that effect.
(b)   A copy or summary of the plan of conversion.
(c)   The statement or statements required by ss. 608.4351-608.43595 concerning availability of appraisal rights, if any, to members of the limited liability company.
(d)   The date on which such notification was mailed or delivered to the members.
(e)   Any other information concerning the plan of conversion.
(5)   The notification required by subsection (3) shall be deemed to be given at the earliest date of:
(a)   The date such notification is received;
(b)   Five days after the date such notification is deposited in the United States mail addressed to the member at the member's address as it appears in the books and records of the limited liability company, with postage thereon prepaid;
(c)   The date shown on the return receipt, if sent by registered or certified mail, return receipt requested, and the receipt is signed by or on behalf of the addressee; or
(d)   The date such notification is given in accordance with the provisions of the articles of organization or the operating agreement of the limited liability company.
(6)   Unless the converting limited liability company's articles of organization or operating agreement or the plan of conversion provides otherwise, notwithstanding the prior approval of the plan of conversion by the managers or members of a converting limited liability company in which management is not reserved to its members, and at any time prior to the filing of the certificate of conversion with the Department of State, the planned conversion may be abandoned, subject to any contractual rights, by such limited liability company by the affirmative vote of a majority of its managers without further action by its members, in accordance with the procedure set forth in the plan of conversion, or if none is set forth in such plan, in the manner determined by the managers of such limited liability company.

History.—
s. 12, ch. 2005-267.

608.4403   Certificate of conversion.—
(1)   After a plan of conversion is approved by a converting limited liability company, the limited liability company shall deliver to the Department of State for filing a certificate of conversion, which shall be executed by the converting limited liability company, and which shall set forth:
(a)   A statement that the limited liability company has been converted into another business entity in compliance with this chapter and that the conversion complies with the law or other applicable law governing the other business entity.
(b)   A statement that the plan of conversion was approved by the converting limited liability company in accordance with this chapter and, if applicable, a statement that the written consent of each member of such limited liability company who, as a result of the conversion, becomes a general partner of the surviving entity has been obtained pursuant to s. 608.4402(2).
(c)   The effective date of the conversion, which, subject to the limitations in s. 608.409(2), may be on or after the date of filing the certificate of conversion, but which shall not be different than the effective date of the conversion under the laws governing the other business entity into which the limited liability company has been converted.
(d)   The address, including street and number, if any, of the principal office of the other business entity under the laws of

the state, country, or jurisdiction in which such entity was organized.

(e)   If the other business entity is a foreign entity and is not authorized to transact business in this state, a statement that the other business entity appoints the Secretary of State as its agent for service of process in a proceeding to enforce obligations of the converting limited liability company, including any appraisal rights of its members under ss. 608.4351-608.43595 and the street and mailing address of an office which the Department of State may use for purposes of s. 48.181.

(f)   A statement that the other business entity has agreed to pay to any members having appraisal rights the amount to which such members are entitled under ss. 608.4351-608.43595.

(2)   A copy of the certificate of conversion, certified by the Department of State, may be filed in the official records of any county in this state in which the converting limited liability company holds an interest in real property.

History.—
s. 12, ch. 2005-267.

608.4404   Effect of conversion.—
When a conversion becomes effective:

(1)   A domestic limited liability company that has been converted into another business entity pursuant to this chapter is for all purposes the same entity that existed before the conversion.

(2)   The title to all real property and other property, or any interest therein, owned by the domestic limited liability company at the time of its conversion into the other business entity remains vested in the converted entity without reversion or impairment by operation of this chapter.

(3)   The other business entity into which the domestic limited liability company was converted shall continue to be responsible and liable for all the liabilities and obligations of such limited liability company, including any liability to members having appraisal rights under ss. 608.4351-608.43595 with respect to such conversion.

(4)   Any claim existing or action or proceeding pending by or against any domestic limited liability company that is converted into another business entity may be continued as if the conversion did not occur. If the converted entity is a foreign entity, such entity shall be deemed to have consented to the jurisdiction of the courts of this state to enforce any obligation of the converting domestic limited liability company if, before the conversion, the converting domestic limited liability company was subject to suit in this state on the obligation. A converted entity that is a foreign entity and not authorized to transact business in this state appoints the Department of State as its agent for service of process for purposes of enforcing an obligation under this subsection, including any appraisal rights of members under ss. 608.4351-608.43595 to the extent applicable to the conversion. Service on the Department of State under this subsection is made in the same manner and with the same consequences as under s. 48.181.

(5)   Neither the rights of creditors nor any liens upon the property of a domestic limited liability company that is converted into another business entity under this chapter shall be impaired by such conversion.

(6)   The member interests, obligations, and other securities, or rights to acquire any member interests, obligations, or other securities, of the domestic limited liability company shall be converted into the shares, partnership interests, interests, obligations, or other securities of the other business entity, including any rights to acquire any such shares, interests, obligations, or other securities, or, in whole or in part, into cash or other consideration as provided in the plan of conversion. The former members of the converting domestic limited liability company shall be entitled only to the rights provided in the plan of conversion and to their appraisal rights, if any, under ss. 608.4351-608.43595 or other applicable law.

History.—
s. 12, ch. 2005-267.

608.441   Dissolution.—
(1)   A limited liability company organized under this chapter shall be dissolved, and the limited liability company's affairs shall be concluded, upon the first to occur of any of the following events:

(a)   At the time specified in the articles of organization or operating agreement, but if no such time is set forth in the articles of organization or operating agreement, then the limited liability company shall have a perpetual existence;

(b)   Upon the occurrence of events specified in the articles of organization or operating agreement;

(c)   Unless otherwise provided in the articles of organization or operating agreement, upon the written consent of all of the members of the limited liability company;

(d)   At any time there are no members; however, unless otherwise provided in the articles of organization or operating agreement, the limited liability company is not dissolved and is not required to be wound up if, within 90 days, or such other period as provided in the articles of organization or operating agreement, after the occurrence of the event that terminated the continued membership of the last remaining member, the personal or other legal representative of the last remaining member agrees in writing to continue the limited liability company and agrees to the admission of the personal representative of such member or its nominee or designee to the limited liability company as a member, effective as of the occurrence of the event that terminated the continued membership of the last remaining member; or

(e)   The entry of an order of dissolution by a circuit court pursuant to subsection (3).

(2)   So long as the limited liability company continues to have at least one remaining member, and except as provided in paragraph (1)(d) or as otherwise provided in the articles of organization or operating agreement, the death, retirement, resignation, expulsion, bankruptcy, or dissolution of any member or the occurrence of any other event that terminates the continued membership of any member shall not cause the limited liability company to be dissolved, and upon the occurrence of any such event, the limited liability company shall be continued without dissolution.

(3)   Unless otherwise provided in the articles of organization or operating agreement, on application by or for a member, the circuit court may order dissolution of a limited liability company if it is established by a preponderance of the evidence that it is not reasonably practicable to carry on the business of the limited liability company in conformity with the articles of organization or the operating agreement.

(4)   Following the occurrence of any of the events specified in this section which cause the dissolution of the limited liability company, the limited liability company shall deliver articles of dissolution to the Department of State for filing.

History.—
s. 2, ch. 82-177; s. 64, ch. 83-216; s. 39, ch. 93-284; s. 1, ch. 99-315; s. 24, ch. 2002-272.

608.4411   Revocation of dissolution.—
(1)   A limited liability company may revoke its dissolution at any time prior to the expiration of 120 days following the effective date of the articles of dissolution.

(2)   Revocation of dissolution shall be authorized in the same manner as the dissolution was authorized.

(3)   After revocation of dissolution is authorized, the limited liability company may revoke the dissolution by delivering articles of revocation of dissolution to the Department of State for filing, together with a copy of its articles of dissolution, that set forth:

(a)   The name of the limited liability company.

(b)   The effective date of the dissolution that was revoked.

(c)   The date that the revocation of dissolution was authorized.

(4)   Revocation of dissolution is effective upon the effective date of the articles of revocation of dissolution.

(5)   When the revocation of dissolution is effective, it relates back to and takes effect as of the effective date of the dissolution and the limited liability company resumes carrying on its business as if dissolution never occurred.

History.—

s. 40, ch. 93-284.

608.4421   Claims against dissolved limited liability company.—

(1)   A dissolved limited liability company may dispose of the known claims against it by following the procedures described in subsections (2), (3), and (4).

(2)   The dissolved limited liability company shall deliver to each of its known claimants written notice of the dissolution at any time after its effective date. The written notice shall:

(a)   Provide a reasonable description of the claim that the claimant may be entitled to assert.

(b)   State whether the claim is admitted or not admitted, in whole or in part, and, if admitted:

1.   The amount that is admitted, which may be as of a given date.

2.   Any interest obligation if fixed by an instrument of indebtedness.

(c)   Provide a mailing address where a claim may be sent.

(d)   State the deadline, which may not be fewer than 120 days after the effective date of the written notice, by which confirmation of the claim must be delivered to the dissolved limited liability company.

(e)   State that the limited liability company may make distributions thereafter to other claimants and its members or former members without further notice.

(3)   A dissolved limited liability company may reject, in whole or in part, any claim made by a claimant pursuant to this subsection by mailing written notice of such rejection to the claimant within 90 days after receipt of such claim and, in all events, at least 150 days before expiration of 3 years following the effective date of dissolution. A notice sent by the limited liability company pursuant to this subsection shall be accompanied by a copy of this section.

(4)   A dissolved limited liability company electing to follow the procedures described in subsections (2) and (3) shall also give notice of the dissolution of the limited liability company to persons with claims contingent upon the occurrence or nonoccurrence of future events or otherwise conditional or unmatured, and request that such persons present such claims in accordance with the terms of such notice. Such notice shall be in substantially the form, and sent in the same manner, as described in subsection (2).

(5)   A dissolved limited liability company shall offer any claimant whose claim is contingent, conditional, or unmatured such security as the limited liability company determines is sufficient to provide compensation to the claimant if the claim matures. The dissolved limited liability company shall deliver such offer to the claimant within 90 days after receipt of such claim and, in all events, at least 150 days before expiration of 3 years following the effective date of dissolution. If the claimant offered such security does not deliver in writing to the dissolved limited liability company a notice rejecting the offer within 120 days after receipt of such offer for security, the claimant is deemed to have accepted such security as the sole source from which to satisfy the claimant's claim against the limited liability company.

(6)   A dissolved limited liability company which has given notice in accordance with subsections (2) and (4) shall petition the circuit court in the county where the limited liability company's principal office is located or was located at the effective date of dissolution to determine the amount and form of security that will be sufficient to provide compensation to any claimant who has rejected the offer for security made pursuant to subsection (5).

(7)   A dissolved limited liability company which has given notice in accordance with subsection (2) shall petition the circuit court in the county where the limited liability company's principal office is located or was located at the effective date of dissolution to determine the amount and form of security which will be sufficient to provide compensation to claimants whose claims are known to the limited liability company but whose identities are unknown. The court shall appoint a guardian ad litem to represent all claimants whose identities are unknown in any proceeding brought under this subsection. The reasonable fees and expenses of such guardian, including all reasonable expert witness fees, shall be paid by the petitioner in such proceeding.

(8)   The giving of any notice or making of any offer pursuant to the provisions of this section shall not revive any claim then barred or constitute acknowledgment by the dissolved limited liability company that any person to whom such notice is sent is a proper claimant and shall not operate as a waiver of any defense or counterclaim in respect of any claim asserted by any person to whom such notice is sent.

(9)   A dissolved limited liability company which has followed the procedures described in subsections (2)-(7):

(a)   Shall pay the claims admitted or made and not rejected in accordance with subsection (3).

(b)   Shall post the security offered and not rejected pursuant to subsection (5).

(c)   Shall post any security ordered by the circuit court in any proceeding under subsections (6) and (7).

(d)   Shall pay or make provision for all other obligations of the limited liability company.

Such claims or obligations shall be paid in full, and any such provision for payments shall be made in full if there are sufficient funds. If there are insufficient funds, such claims and obligations shall be paid or provided for according to their priority and, among claims of equal priority, ratably to the extent of funds legally available therefor. Any remaining funds shall be distributed pursuant to s. 608.444; however, such distribution may not be made before the expiration of 150 days from the date of the last notice of rejections given pursuant to subsection (3).

(10)   A dissolved limited liability company which has not followed the procedures described in subsections (2) and (3) shall pay or make reasonable provision to pay all claims and obligations, including all contingent, conditional, or unmatured claims known to the limited liability company and all claims which are known to the dissolved limited liability company but for which the identity of the claimant is unknown. Such claims shall be paid in full, and any such provision for payment made shall be made in full if there are sufficient funds. If there are insufficient funds, such claims and obligations shall be paid or provided for according to their priority and, among claims of equal priority, ratably to the extent of funds legally available therefor. Any remaining funds shall be distributed pursuant to s. 608.444.

(11)   A member of a dissolved limited liability company, the assets of which were distributed pursuant to subsection (9) or subsection (10) is not liable for any claim against the limited liability company in an amount in excess of such member's pro rata share of the claim or the amount distributed to the member, whichever is less.

(12)   A member of a dissolved limited liability company, the assets of which were distributed pursuant to subsection (9) is not liable for any claim against the limited liability company on which a proceeding is not begun prior to the expiration of 3 years following the effective date of dissolution.

(13)   The aggregate liability of any member of a dissolved limited liability company for claims against the dissolved limited liability company may not exceed the amount distributed to the member in dissolution.

History.—

s. 41, ch. 93-284; s. 60, ch. 97-102; s. 1, ch. 99-315.

608.4431   Effect of dissolution.—

(1)   A dissolved limited liability company continues its existence but may not carry on any business except that appropriate to wind up and liquidate its business and affairs, including:

(a)   Collecting its assets.

(b)   Disposing of its properties that will not be distributed in kind to its members.

(c)   Discharging or making provision for discharging its liabilities.

(d)   Distributing its assets in accordance with s. 608.444.

(e)   Doing every other act necessary to wind up and liquidate its business and affairs.

(2)   Dissolution of a limited liability company does not:

(a)   Transfer title to the limited liability company assets.

(b)   Prevent commencement of a proceeding by or against the limited liability company in its name.

(c)   Abate or suspend a proceeding pending by or against the limited liability company on the effective date of dissolution.

(d)   Terminate the authority of the registered agent of the limited liability company.

(3)   The name of the dissolved limited liability company shall not be available for assumption or use by another limited liability company until 120 days after the effective date of dissolution.

History.—

s. 42, ch. 93-284.

608.444   Distribution of assets upon dissolution.—

In settling accounts after dissolution of a limited liability company, the assets of the limited liability company must be distributed in the following order:

(1)   To creditors, including members who are creditors, to the extent permitted by law in satisfaction of liabilities of the limited liability company, whether by payment or establishment of reserves, other than liabilities for distributions to members under s. 608.426 or s. 608.427.

(2)   Except as provided in the operating agreement, to members and former members in satisfaction of liabilities for distributions under s. 608.426 or s. 608.427.

(3)   Except as provided in the articles of organization or the operating agreement, to members pro rata in proportion to their then-current percentage, or other interests in the profits, of the limited liability company.

History.—

s. 2, ch. 82-177; s. 43, ch. 93-284; s. 1, ch. 99-315; s. 25, ch. 2002-272.

608.445   Articles of dissolution.—

The articles of dissolution shall set forth:

(1)   The name of the limited liability company.

(2)   The effective date of the limited liability company's dissolution.

(3)   A description of the occurrence that resulted in the limited liability company's dissolution pursuant to s. 608.441.

(4)   The fact that all debts, obligations, and liabilities of the limited liability company have been paid or discharged, or that adequate provision has been made therefor pursuant to s. 608.4421.

(5)   The fact that all the remaining property and assets have been distributed among its members in accordance with their respective rights and interests.

(6)   The fact that there are no suits pending against the limited liability company in any court or that adequate provision has been made for the satisfaction of any judgment, order, or decree which may be entered against it in any pending suit.

History.—

s. 2, ch. 82-177; s. 67, ch. 83-216; s. 44, ch. 93-284; s. 26, ch. 2002-272.

608.446   Filing of articles of dissolution.—

(1)   The articles of dissolution of the limited liability company shall be delivered to the Department of State. If the Department of State finds that such articles of dissolution conform to law, it shall, when all fees and license taxes have been paid as prescribed in this chapter, file the articles of dissolution.

(2)   The certificate of dissolution shall be returned to the representative of the dissolved limited liability company. Upon the issuance of such certificate of dissolution, the existence of the limited liability company shall cease, except for the purpose of suits, other proceedings, and appropriate action as provided in this chapter. The manager or managers in office at the time of dissolution, or the survivors of them, or, if none, the members, shall thereafter be trustees for the members and creditors of the dissolved limited liability company; and as such the trustees shall have authority to distribute any property of the limited liability company discovered after dissolution, to convey real estate, and to take such other action as may be necessary on behalf of and in the name of such dissolved limited liability company.

History.—

s. 2, ch. 82-177; s. 68, ch. 83-216; s. 45, ch. 93-284; s. 27, ch. 2002-272.

608.447   Cancellation of articles of organization.—

The articles of organization of a limited liability company shall be canceled by the Department of State upon issuance of the certificate of dissolution.

History.—

s. 2, ch. 82-177; s. 69, ch. 83-216; s. 1, ch. 99-315.

608.448   Grounds for administrative dissolution.—

(1)   The Department of State may commence a proceeding under s. 608.4481 to administratively dissolve a limited liability company if:

(a)   The limited liability company has failed to file its annual report or pay the annual report filing fee within the time required by this chapter.

(b)   The limited liability company is without a registered agent or registered office in this state for 30 days or more.

(c)   The limited liability company does not notify the Department of State within 30 days that its registered agent or registered office has been changed, that its registered agent has resigned, or that its registered office has been discontinued.

(d)   The limited liability company has failed to answer truthfully and fully, within 30 days after mailing or within such additional time as fixed by the Department of State, interrogatories propounded by the Department of State.

(e)   The limited liability company's period of duration has expired.

(2)   The enumeration in subsection (1) of grounds for administrative dissolution shall not exclude actions or special proceedings by the Department of Legal Affairs or any state officials for the annulment or dissolution of a limited liability company for other causes as provided in any other law of this state.

History.—

s. 2, ch. 82-177; s. 46, ch. 93-284; s. 1, ch. 99-315.

608.4481   Procedure for and effect of administrative dissolution.—

(1)   If the Department of State determines that one or more grounds exist under s. 608.448 for dissolving a limited liability company, it shall serve the limited liability company with written notice of its determination, stating the grounds therefor.

(2) If the limited liability company does not correct each ground for dissolution or demonstrate to the reasonable satisfaction of the Department of State that each ground determined by the Department of State does not exist within 60 days after issuance of the notice, the Department of State shall administratively dissolve the limited liability company by issuing a certificate of dissolution that recites the ground or grounds for dissolution and its effective date.

(3) A limited liability company administratively dissolved continues its existence but may not carry on any business except that necessary to wind up and liquidate its business and affairs under s. 608.4431 and notify claimants under s. 608.4421.

(4) A manager or member of a limited liability company dissolved pursuant to this section, purporting to act on behalf of the limited liability company, is personally liable for the debts, obligations, and liabilities of the limited liability company arising from such action and incurred subsequent to the limited liability company's administrative dissolution only if the manager or member has actual notice of the administrative dissolution at the time such action is taken; but such liability shall be terminated upon the ratification of such action by the limited liability company's members subsequent to the reinstatement of the limited liability company under s. 608.4482.

(5) The administrative dissolution of a limited liability company does not terminate the authority of its registered agent.
History.—
s. 47, ch. 93-284; s. 61, ch. 97-102; s. 1, ch. 99-315.

608.4482 Reinstatement following administrative dissolution.—
(1)(a) A limited liability company administratively dissolved under s. 608.4481 may apply to the Department of State for reinstatement at any time after the effective date of dissolution. The application shall:
1. Recite the name of the limited liability company and the effective date of its administrative dissolution.
2. State that the ground or grounds for dissolution either did not exist or have been eliminated and that no further grounds currently exist for dissolution.
3. State that the limited liability company's name satisfies the requirements of s. 608.406.
4. State that all fees owed by the limited liability company and computed at the rate provided by law at the time the limited liability company applies for reinstatement have been paid.
(b) As an alternative to the procedures of paragraph (a), an administratively dissolved limited liability company may submit a current annual report, signed by the registered agent, which substantially complies with the requirements of paragraph (a).
(2) If the Department of State determines that the application contains the information required by subsection (1) and that the information is correct, it shall cancel the certificate of dissolution and prepare a certificate of reinstatement that recites its determination and the effective date of reinstatement, file the original of the certificate, and serve a copy on the limited liability company.
(3) When the reinstatement is effective, it relates back to and takes effect as of the effective date of the administrative dissolution and the limited liability company resumes carrying on its business as if the administrative dissolution had never occurred.
(4) The name of the dissolved limited liability company shall not be available for assumption or use by another limited liability company until 1 year after the effective date of dissolution unless the dissolved limited liability company provides the Department of State with an affidavit executed as required

by s. 608.408 permitting the immediate assumption or use of the name by another limited liability company.
History.—
s. 48, ch. 93-284.

608.4483 Appeal from denial or reinstatement.—
(1) If the Department of State denies a limited liability company's application for reinstatement following administrative dissolution, it shall serve the limited liability company with a written notice that explains the reason or reasons for denial.
(2) After exhaustion of administrative remedies, the limited liability company may appeal the denial of reinstatement to the appropriate court as provided in s. 120.68 within 30 days after service of the notice of denial is perfected. The limited liability company appeals by petitioning the court to set aside the dissolution and attaching to the petition copies of the Department of State's certificate of dissolution, the limited liability company's application for reinstatement, and the department's notice of denial.
(3) The court may summarily order the Department of State to reinstate the dissolved limited liability company or may take other action the court considers appropriate.
(4) The court's final decision may be appealed as in other civil proceedings.
History.—
s. 49, ch. 93-284; s. 265, ch. 96-410.

608.449 Grounds for judicial dissolution.—
A circuit court may dissolve a limited liability company:
(1)(a) In a proceeding by the Department of Legal Affairs if it is established that:
1. The limited liability company obtained its articles of organization through fraud; or
2. The limited liability company has continued to exceed or abuse the authority conferred upon it by law.
(b) The enumeration in paragraph (a) of grounds for involuntary dissolution does not exclude actions or special proceedings by the Department of Legal Affairs or any state official for the annulment or dissolution of a limited liability company for other causes as provided in any other law of this state.
(2) In a proceeding by a manager or member if it is established that:
(a) The managers, managing members, or members are deadlocked in the management of the limited liability company affairs, the members are unable to break the deadlock, and irreparable injury to the limited liability company is threatened or being suffered; or
(b) The limited liability company's assets are being misappropriated or wasted.
(3) In a proceeding by a creditor if it is established that:
(a) The creditor's claim has been reduced to judgment, the execution on that judgment returned unsatisfied, and the limited liability company is insolvent; or
(b) The limited liability company has admitted in writing that the creditor's claim is due and owing and the limited liability company is insolvent.
(4) In a proceeding by the limited liability company to have its voluntary dissolution continued under court supervision.
History.—
s. 2, ch. 82-177; s. 50, ch. 93-284; s. 1, ch. 99-315; s. 28, ch. 2002-272.

608.4491 Procedure for judicial dissolution.—
(1) Venue for a proceeding brought under s. 608.449 lies in the circuit court of the county where the limited liability company's principal office is or was last located, as shown by the records of the Department of State, or, if none in this state, where its registered office is or was last located.
(2) It is not necessary to make members parties to a proceeding to dissolve a limited liability company unless relief is sought against them individually.

(3)   A court in a proceeding brought to dissolve a limited liability company may issue injunctions, appoint a receiver or custodian pendente lite with all powers and duties the court directs, take other action required to preserve the limited liability company's assets wherever located, and carry on the business of the limited liability company until a full hearing can be held.

History.—

s. 51, ch. 93-284.

608.4492   Receivership or custodianship.—

(1)   A court in a judicial proceeding brought to dissolve a limited liability company may appoint one or more receivers to wind up and liquidate, or one or more custodians to manage, the business and affairs of the limited liability company. The court shall hold a hearing, after notifying all parties to the proceeding and any interested persons designated by the court, before appointing a receiver or custodian. The court appointing a receiver or custodian has exclusive jurisdiction over the limited liability company and all of its property wherever located.

(2)   The court may appoint a person authorized to act as a receiver or custodian. The court may require the receiver or custodian to post bond, with or without sureties, in an amount the court directs.

(3)   The court shall describe the powers and duties of the receiver or custodian in its appointing order, which may be amended from time to time. Among other powers:

(a)   The receiver:

1.   May dispose of all or any part of the assets of the limited liability company wherever located, at a public or private sale, if authorized by the court.

2.   May sue and defend in the receiver's own name as receiver of the limited liability company in all courts of this state.

(b)   The custodian may exercise all of the powers of the limited liability company, through or in place of its managers or members, to the extent necessary to manage the affairs of the limited liability company in the best interests of its members and creditors.

(4)   The court during a receivership may redesignate the receiver a custodian, and during a custodianship may redesignate the custodian a receiver, if doing so is in the best interests of the limited liability company and its members and creditors.

(5)   The court from time to time during the receivership or custodianship may order compensation paid and expense disbursements or reimbursements made to the receiver or custodian and the receiver's or custodian's counsel from the assets of the limited liability company or proceeds from the sale of assets.

(6)   The court has jurisdiction to appoint an ancillary receiver for the assets and business of a limited liability company. The ancillary receiver shall serve ancillary to a receiver located in any other state, whenever the court deems that circumstances exist requiring the appointment of such a receiver. The court may appoint such an ancillary receiver for a foreign limited liability company even though no receiver has been appointed elsewhere. Such receivership shall be converted into an ancillary receivership when an order entered by a court of competent jurisdiction in the other state provides for a receivership of the limited liability company.

History.—

s. 52, ch. 93-284; s. 62, ch. 97-102; s. 1, ch. 99-315.

608.4493   Decree of dissolution.—

(1)   If after a hearing the court determines that one or more grounds for judicial dissolution described in s. 608.449 exist, it may enter a decree dissolving the limited liability company and specifying the effective date of the dissolution, and the clerk of the court shall deliver a certified copy of the decree to the Department of State, which shall file it.

(2)   After entering the decree of dissolution, the court shall direct the winding up and liquidation of the limited liability company's business and affairs in accordance with s. 608.4431 and the notification of claimants in accordance with s. 608.4421, subject to the provisions of subsection (3).

(3)   In a proceeding for judicial dissolution, the court may require all creditors of the limited liability company to file with the clerk of the court or with the receiver, in such form as the court may prescribe, proofs under oath of their respective claims. If the court requires the filing of claims, it shall fix a date, which shall not be less than 4 months from the date of the order, as the last day for filing of claims. The court shall prescribe the deadline for filing claims that shall be given to creditors and claimants. Prior to the date so fixed, the court may extend the time for the filing of claims by court order. Creditors and claimants failing to file proofs of claim on or before the date so fixed may be barred, by order of court, from participating in the distribution of the assets of the limited liability company. Nothing in this section affects the enforceability of any recorded mortgage or lien or the perfected security interest or rights of a person in possession of real or personal property.

History.—

s. 53, ch. 93-284.

608.4511   Annual report for Department of State.—

(1)   Each domestic limited liability company and each foreign limited liability company authorized to transact business in this state shall deliver to the Department of State for filing a sworn annual report on such forms as the Department of State prescribes that sets forth:

(a)   The name of the limited liability company and the state or country under the law of which it is organized.

(b)   The date of organization or, if a foreign limited liability company, the date on which it was admitted to do business in this state.

(c)   The street address and the mailing address of its principal office.

(d)   The limited liability company's federal employer identification number or, if none, whether one has been applied for.

(e)   The names and business, residence, or mailing address of its managing members or managers.

(f)   The street address of its registered office and the name of its registered agent at that office in this state.

(g)   Such additional information as may be necessary or appropriate to enable the Department of State to carry out the provisions of this chapter.

(2)   Proof to the satisfaction of the Department of State that on or before May 1 such report was deposited in the United States mail in a sealed envelope, properly addressed with postage prepaid, shall be deemed timely compliance with this requirement.

(3)   If an annual report does not contain the information required by this section, the Department of State shall promptly notify the reporting domestic or foreign limited liability company in writing and return the report to it for correction. If the report is corrected to contain the information required by this section and delivered to the Department of State within 30 days after the effective date of notice, it is deemed to be timely filed.

(4)   Each report shall be executed by the limited liability company by a managing member or manager or, if the limited liability company is in the hands of a receiver or trustee, shall be executed on behalf of the limited liability company by such receiver or trustee, and the signing thereof shall have the same legal effect as if made under oath, without the necessity of appending such oath thereto.

(5)   The first annual report shall be delivered to the Department of State between January 1 and May 1 of the year

following the calendar year in which a domestic limited liability company was organized or a foreign limited liability company was authorized to transact business. Subsequent annual reports shall be delivered to the Department of State between January 1 and May 1 of the subsequent calendar years.

(6)   Information in the annual report shall be current as of the date the annual report is executed on behalf of the limited liability company.

(7)   Any limited liability company failing to file an annual report which complies with the requirements of this section shall not be permitted to prosecute, maintain, or defend any action in any court of this state until such report is filed and all fees, penalties, and taxes due under this chapter are paid and shall be subject to dissolution or cancellation of its certificate of authority to do business as provided in this chapter.

(8)   The department shall prescribe the forms on which to make the annual report called for in this section and may substitute the uniform business report, pursuant to s. 606.06, as a means of satisfying the requirement of this part.

History.—
s. 55, ch. 93-284; s. 7, ch. 99-218; s. 1, ch. 99-315.

608.452   Fees of the Department of State.—
The fees of the Department of State under this chapter are as follows:

(1)   For furnishing a certified copy, $30.

(2)   For filing original articles of organization, articles of revocation of dissolution, or a foreign limited liability company's application for a certificate of authority to transact business, $100.

(3)   For filing a certificate of merger of limited liability companies or other business entities, $25 per constituent party to the merger, unless a specific fee is required for a party in other applicable law.

(4)   For filing an annual report, $50.

(5)   For filing an application for reinstatement after an administrative or judicial dissolution or a revocation of authority to transact business, $100.

(6)   For filing a certificate designating a registered agent or changing a registered agent, $25.

(7)   For filing a registered agent's statement of resignation from an active limited liability company, $85.

(8)   For filing a registered agent's statement of resignation from a dissolved limited liability company, $25.

(9)   For filing a certificate of conversion of a limited liability company, $25.

(10)   For filing any other limited liability company document, $25.

(11)   For furnishing a certificate of status, $5.

History.—
s. 2, ch. 82-177; s. 70, ch. 83-216; s. 65, ch. 90-132; s. 27, ch. 92-319; s. 56, ch. 93-284; s. 1, ch. 99-315; s. 13, ch. 2005-267.

608.455   Waiver of notice.—
When, under the provisions of this chapter or under the provisions of the articles of organization or operating agreement of a limited liability company, notice is required to be given to a member of a limited liability company or to a manager of a limited liability company having a manager or managers, a waiver in writing signed by the person or persons entitled to the notice, whether made before or after the time for notice to be given, is equivalent to the giving of notice.

History.—
s. 2, ch. 82-177; s. 72, ch. 83-216; s. 57, ch. 93-284; s. 1, ch. 99-315.

608.461   Jurisdiction of the circuit court.—
The circuit courts shall have jurisdiction to enforce the provisions of this chapter.

History.—
s. 2, ch. 82-177.

608.462   Parties to actions by or against limited liability company.—
A member of a limited liability company is not a proper party to proceedings by or against a limited liability company, except when the object is to enforce a member's right against, or liability to, the limited liability company.

History.—
s. 2, ch. 82-177.

608.463   Service of process.—
(1)   Process against a limited liability company may be served:

(a)   In accordance with chapter 48 or chapter 49, as if the limited liability company were a partnership.

(b)   Upon the registered agent at the agent's street address.

(2)   Any notice to or demand on a limited liability company organized pursuant to this chapter may be made:

(a)   By delivery to a manager of the limited liability company, if the management of the limited liability company is vested in one or more managers, or by delivery to a member, if the management of the limited liability company is vested in the members.

(b)   By mailing a writing, which notice or demand in writing is mailed to the registered office of the limited liability company in this state or to another address in this state which is the principal office of the limited liability company.

(3)   Nothing contained in this section shall limit or affect the right to serve, in any other manner now or hereafter permitted by law, any process, notice, or demand required or permitted by law to be served upon a limited liability company.

History.—
s. 2, ch. 82-177; s. 64, ch. 97-102; s. 1, ch. 99-315; s. 29, ch. 2002-272.

608.471   Tax exemption on income of certain limited liability companies.—
(1)   A limited liability company classified as a partnership for federal income tax purposes, or a single member limited liability company which is disregarded as an entity separate from its owner for federal income tax purposes, and organized pursuant to this chapter or qualified to do business in this state as a foreign limited liability company is not an "artificial entity" within the purview of s. 220.02 and is not subject to the tax imposed under chapter 220. If a single member limited liability company is disregarded as an entity separate from its owner for federal income tax purposes, its activities are, for purposes of taxation under chapter 220, treated in the same manner as a sole proprietorship, branch, or division of the owner.

(2)   For purposes of taxation under chapter 220, a limited liability company formed in this state or authorized to transact business in this state as a foreign limited liability company shall be classified as a partnership, or a limited liability company which has only one member shall be disregarded as an entity separate from its owner for federal income tax purposes, unless classified otherwise for federal income tax purposes, in which case the limited liability company shall be classified identically to its classification for federal income tax purposes. For purposes of taxation under chapter 220, a member or an assignee of a member of a limited liability company formed in this state or qualified to do business in this state as a foreign limited liability company shall be treated as a resident or nonresident partner unless classified otherwise for federal income tax purposes, in which case the member or assignee of a member shall have the same status as such member or assignee of a member has for federal income tax purposes.

(3)   Single-member limited liability companies and other entities that are disregarded for federal income tax purposes must be treated as separate legal entities for all non-income-

tax purposes. The Department of Revenue shall adopt rules to take into account that single-member disregarded entities such as limited liability companies and qualified subchapter S corporations may be disregarded as separate entities for federal tax purposes and therefore may report and account for income, employment, and other taxes under the taxpayer identification number of the owner of the single-member entity.

History.—

s. 2, ch. 82-177; s. 73, ch. 83-216; s. 58, ch. 93-284; s. 14, ch. 98-101; s. 1, ch. 99-315; s. 53, ch. 2002-218.

608.501 Foreign limited liability company; authority to transact business required.—

(1)   A foreign limited liability company may not transact business in this state until it obtains a certificate of authority from the Department of State.

(2)   The following activities, among others, do not constitute transacting business within the meaning of subsection (1):

(a)   Maintaining, defending, or settling any proceeding.

(b)   Holding meetings of the managers or members or carrying on other activities concerning internal company affairs.

(c)   Maintaining bank accounts.

(d)   Maintaining managers or agencies for the transfer, exchange, and registration of the limited liability company's own securities or maintaining trustees or depositaries with respect to those securities.

(e)   Selling through independent contractors.

(f)   Soliciting or obtaining orders, whether by mail or through employees, agents or otherwise, if the orders require acceptance outside this state before they become contracts.

(g)   Creating or acquiring indebtedness, mortgages, and security interests in real or personal property.

(h)   Securing or collecting debts or enforcing mortgages and security interests in property securing the debts.

(i)   Transacting business in interstate commerce.

(j)   Conducting an isolated transaction that is completed within 30 days and that is not one in the course of repeated transactions of a like nature.

(k)   Owning and controlling a subsidiary corporation or limited liability company incorporated in or transacting business within this state or voting the stock of any corporation which it has lawfully acquired.

(l)   Owning a limited partnership interest in a limited partnership that is doing business within this state, unless such limited partner manages or controls the partnership or exercises the powers and duties of a general partner.

(m)   Owning, without more, real or personal property.

(3)   The list of activities in subsection (2) is not exhaustive.

(4)   This section has no application to the question of whether any foreign limited liability company is subject to service of process and suit in this state under any law of this state.

History.—

s. 59, ch. 93-284.

608.502 Consequences of transacting business without authority.—

(1)   A foreign limited liability company transacting business in this state without a certificate of authority may not maintain a proceeding in any court in this state until it obtains a certificate of authority.

(2)   The successor to a foreign limited liability company that transacted business in this state without a certificate of authority and the assignee of a cause of action arising out of that business may not maintain a proceeding based on that cause of action in any court in this state until the foreign limited liability company or its successor obtains a certificate of authority.

(3)   A court may stay a proceeding commenced by a foreign limited liability company or its successor or assignee until it determines whether the foreign limited liability company or its successor requires a certificate of authority. If it so determines, the court may further stay the proceeding until the foreign limited liability company or its successor obtains the certificate.

(4)   A foreign limited liability company which transacts business in this state without authority to do so shall be liable to this state for the years or parts thereof during which it transacted business in this state without authority in an amount equal to all fees, penalties, and taxes which would have been imposed by this chapter upon such limited liability company had it duly applied for and received authority to transact business in this state as required by this chapter. In addition to the payments thus prescribed, such limited liability company shall be liable for a civil penalty of not less than $500 or more than $1,000 for each year or part thereof during which it transacts business in this state without a certificate of authority. The Department of State may collect all penalties due under this subsection.

(5)   Notwithstanding subsections (1) and (2), the failure of a foreign limited liability company to obtain a certificate of authority does not impair the validity of any of its contracts, deeds, mortgages, security interests, or acts or prevent it from defending any proceeding in this state.

(6)   A member or a manager of a foreign limited liability company is not liable for the obligations of the foreign limited liability company solely by reason of the limited liability company's having transacted business in this state without a certificate of authority.

(7)   If a foreign limited liability company transacts business in this state without a certificate of authority, the foreign limited liability company appoints the Secretary of State as its agent for substitute service of process pursuant to s. 48.181 for claims arising out of the transaction of business in this state.

History.—

s. 60, ch. 93-284; s. 1, ch. 99-315.

608.503 Application for certificate of authority.—

(1)   A foreign limited liability company may apply for a certificate of authority to transact business in this state by delivering an application to the Department of State for filing. Such application shall be made on forms prescribed and furnished by the Department of State and shall set forth:

(a)   The name of the foreign limited liability company, which shall satisfy the requirements of s. 608.506.

(b)   The jurisdiction under the law of which it is organized.

(c)   Its date of organization and period of duration.

(d)   The street address of its principal office.

(e)   The street address of its registered office in this state and the name of its registered agent at that office.

(f)   Whether or not the limited liability company is manager-managed and, if so, the usual business addresses of its managing members or managers.

(g)   The nature of the business or purposes to be conducted or promoted in this state.

(h)   Such additional information as may be necessary or appropriate in order to enable the Department of State to determine whether such limited liability company is entitled to file an application for authority to transact business in this state and to determine and assess the fees, penalties, and taxes payable as prescribed in this chapter.

(2)   The foreign limited liability company shall deliver with the completed application a certificate of existence, or a document of similar import, duly authenticated by the official having custody of records in the jurisdiction under the law of which it is organized, not more than 90 days prior to delivery of the application to the Department of State. A translation of the certificate, under oath of the translator, shall be attached to a certificate which is in a language other than the English language.

(3) A foreign limited liability company shall not be denied authority to transact business in this state by reason of the fact that the laws of the jurisdiction under which such limited liability company is organized governing its organization and internal affairs differ from the laws of this state.

History.—

s. 61, ch. 93-284; s. 1, ch. 99-315.

608.504 Amended certificate of authority.—

(1) A foreign limited liability company authorized to transact business in this state shall make application to the Department of State to obtain an amended certificate of authority if any statement in the limited liability company's application was false or becomes false due to change in circumstances or if the foreign limited liability company changes:

(a) Its limited liability company name.

(b) The period of its duration.

(c) The jurisdiction of its organization.

(2) Such application shall be made within 30 days after the occurrence of any change set forth in subsection (1), shall be made on forms prescribed by the Department of State, shall be executed and filed in the same manner as an original application for authority, and shall set forth:

(a) The name of the foreign limited liability company as it appears on the records of the Department of State.

(b) The jurisdiction of its organization.

(c) The date it was authorized to do business in this state.

(d) If the name of the foreign limited liability company has been changed, the name relinquished, the new name, a statement that the change of name has been effected under the laws of the jurisdiction of its organization, and the date the change was effected.

(e) If the amendment changes its period of duration, a statement of such change.

(f) If the amendment changes the jurisdiction of its organization, a statement of such change.

(3) The requirements of s. 608.503 for obtaining an original certificate of authority apply to obtaining an amended certificate under this section.

History.—

s. 62, ch. 93-284; s. 1, ch. 99-315; s. 30, ch. 2002-272.

608.505 Effect of certificate of authority.—

(1) A certificate of authority authorizes the foreign limited liability company to which it is issued to transact business in this state subject, however, to the right of the Department of State to suspend or revoke the certificate as provided in this chapter.

(2) A foreign limited liability company with a valid certificate of authority has the same but no greater rights and privileges than a domestic limited liability company. Unless otherwise provided by this chapter, a foreign limited liability company is subject to the same duties, restrictions, penalties, and liabilities now or later imposed on, a domestic limited liability company of like character.

(3) This chapter does not authorize this state to regulate the organization or internal affairs of a foreign limited liability company authorized to transact business in this state. The laws of the state or other jurisdiction under which a foreign limited liability company is organized govern the foreign limited liability company's organization, internal affairs, and the liability of its managers, members, and their transferees.

History.—

s. 63, ch. 93-284; s. 1, ch. 99-315.

608.506 Name of foreign limited liability company.—

(1) A foreign limited liability company is not entitled to file an application for a certificate of authority unless the name of such limited liability company satisfies the requirements of s. 608.406. If the limited liability company name of a foreign limited liability company does not satisfy the requirements of

s. 608.406, the foreign limited liability company, to obtain or maintain a certificate of authority to transact business in this state may use a fictitious name to transact business in this state if it delivers to the Department of State for filing a copy of the consent of its managing members or managers, adopting the fictitious name. The fictitious name adopted shall satisfy the requirements of s. 608.406.

(2) If a foreign limited liability company authorized to transact business in this state changes its corporate name to one that does not satisfy the requirements of s. 608.406, it may not transact business in this state under the changed name until it adopts a name satisfying the requirements of s. 608.406 and obtains an amended certificate of authority under s. 608.504.

History.—

s. 64, ch. 93-284.

608.507 Registered office and registered agent of foreign limited liability company.—

Each foreign limited liability company in this state must continuously maintain in this state:

(1) A registered office that may be the same as any of its places of business.

(2) A registered agent, which may be either:

(a) An individual who resides in this state and whose business office is identical with the registered office; or

(b) A foreign or domestic entity authorized to transact business in this state which has a business office identical with the registered office.

History.—

s. 65, ch. 93-284; s. 1, ch. 99-315; s. 31, ch. 2002-272.

608.508 Change of registered office and registered agent of foreign limited liability company.—

(1) A foreign limited liability company authorized to transact business in this state may change its registered office or registered agent by delivering to the Department of State for filing a statement of change which satisfies the requirements of s. 608.408 and sets forth:

(a) Its name.

(b) The street address of its current registered office.

(c) If the current registered office is to be changed, the street address of its new registered office.

(d) The name of its current registered agent.

(e) If the current registered agent is to be changed, the name of its new registered agent and the new agent's written consent, either on the statement or attached to it, to the appointment.

(f) That, after the change or changes are made, the street address of its registered office and the business office of its registered agent will be identical.

(2) If a registered agent changes the street address of such agent's business office, the registered agent may change the street address of the registered office of any foreign limited liability company for which the agent is the registered agent by notifying the limited liability company in writing of the change and signing, either manually or in facsimile, and delivering to the Department of State for filing a statement of change that complies with the requirements of paragraphs (1)(a)-(f) and recites that the limited liability company has been notified of the change.

History.—

s. 66, ch. 93-284; s. 65, ch. 97-102; s. 1, ch. 99-315.

608.509 Resignation of registered agent or foreign limited liability company.—

(1) The registered agent of a foreign limited liability company may resign his or her agency appointment by signing and delivering to the Department of State for filing the original statement of resignation and mailing a copy of such statement to the limited liability company at the limited liability

company's principal office address shown in its most recent annual report or, if none, shown in its certificate of authority or most recently filed document. This statement of resignation shall state that a copy of such statement has been mailed to the limited liability company at the address so stated. The statement of resignation may include a statement that the registered office is also discontinued.

(2)   The agency appointment is terminated, and the registered office discontinued if so provided, on the 31st day after the date on which the statement was filed.

History.—
s. 67, ch. 93-284; s. 66, ch. 97-102.

608.5101   Service of process; notice or demand on a foreign limited liability company.—

(1)   The registered agent of a foreign limited liability company authorized to transact business in this state is the limited liability company's agent for service of process, notice, or demand required or permitted by law to be served on the foreign limited liability company.

(2)   A foreign limited liability company may be served by registered or certified mail, return receipt requested, addressed to the secretary of the foreign limited liability company at its principal office shown in its application for a certificate of authority or in its most recent annual report if the foreign limited liability company:

(a)   Has no registered agent or its registered agent cannot with reasonable diligence be served;

(b)   Has withdrawn from transacting business in this state under s. 608.511; or

(c)   Has had its certificate of authority revoked under s. 608.513.

(3)   Service is perfected under subsection (2) at the earliest of:

(a)   The date the foreign limited liability company receives the mail.

(b)   The date shown on the return receipt, if signed on behalf of the foreign limited liability company.

(c)   Five days after its deposit in the United States mail, as evidenced by the postmark, if mailed postpaid and correctly addressed.

(4)   This section does not prescribe the only means, or necessarily the required means, of serving a foreign limited liability company. Process against any foreign limited liability company may also be served in accordance with chapter 48 or chapter 49.

History.—
s. 68, ch. 93-284.

608.511   Withdrawal of foreign limited liability company.—

(1)   A foreign limited liability company authorized to transact business in this state may not withdraw from this state until it obtains a certificate of withdrawal from the Department of State.

(2)   A foreign limited liability company authorized to transact business in this state may apply for a certificate of withdrawal by delivering an application to the Department of State for filing. The application shall be made on forms prescribed and furnished by the Department of State and shall set forth:

(a)   The name of the foreign limited liability company and the jurisdiction under the law of which it is organized.

(b)   That it is not transacting business in this state and that it surrenders its authority to transact business in this state.

(c)   That it revokes the authority of its registered agent to accept service on its behalf and appoints the Department of State as its agent for service of process based on a cause of action arising during the time it was authorized to transact business in this state.

(d)   A mailing address to which the Department of State may mail a copy of any process served on it under paragraph (c).

(e)   A commitment to notify the Department of State in the future of any change in its mailing address.

(3)   After the withdrawal of the limited liability company is effective, service of process on the Department of State under this section is service on the foreign limited liability company. Upon receipt of the process, the Department of State shall mail a copy of the process to the foreign limited liability company at the mailing address set forth under subsection (2).

History.—
s. 69, ch. 93-284.

608.512   Grounds for revocation of authority to transact business.—

The Department of State may commence a proceeding under s. 608.513 to revoke the certificate of authority of a foreign limited liability company authorized to transact business in this state if:

(1)   The foreign limited liability company has failed to file its annual report with the Department of State within the time required by this chapter.

(2)   The foreign limited liability company does not pay, within the time required by this chapter, any fees, taxes, or penalties imposed by this chapter or other law.

(3)   The foreign limited liability company is without a registered agent or registered office in this state for 30 days or more.

(4)   The foreign limited liability company does not notify the Department of State under s. 608.508 or s. 608.509 that its registered agent has resigned or that its registered office has been discontinued within 30 days after the resignation or discontinuance.

(5)   The foreign limited liability company's period of duration has expired.

(6)   A member, manager, or agent of the foreign limited liability company signed a document the member, manager, or agent knew was false in any material respect with intent that the document be delivered to the Department of State for filing.

(7)   The Department of State receives a duly authenticated certificate from the other official having custody of records in the jurisdiction under the law of which the foreign limited liability company is incorporated stating that it has been dissolved or disappeared as a result of a merger.

(8)   The foreign limited liability company has failed to answer truthfully and fully, within the time prescribed in s. 608.448, interrogatories propounded by the Department of State.

(9)   The foreign limited liability company failed to amend its certificate of authority as required by s. 608.504.

History.—
s. 70, ch. 93-284; s. 67, ch. 97-102; s. 1, ch. 99-315.

608.513   Procedure for and effect of revocation.—

(1)   If the Department of State determines that one or more grounds exist under s. 608.512 for revocation of a certificate of authority, the Department of State shall serve the foreign limited liability company with written notice of such determination under s. 608.5101.

(2)   If the foreign limited liability company does not correct each ground for revocation or demonstrate to the reasonable satisfaction of the Department of State that each ground determined by the Department of State does not exist within 60 days after issuance of notice is perfected under s. 608.5101, the Department of State shall revoke the foreign limited liability company's certificate of authority by signing a certificate of revocation that recites the ground or grounds for revocation and its effective date.

(3)   The authority of a foreign limited liability company to transact business in this state ceases on the date shown on the certificate revoking its certificate of authority.

(4)   Revocation of a foreign limited liability company's certificate of authority does not terminate the authority of the
registered agent of the limited liability company.
History.—
s. 71, ch. 93-284.

608.5135 Revocation; application for reinstatement.—
(1)(a)   If the certificate of authority of a limited liability
company has been revoked, the foreign limited liability company may apply to the Department of State for reinstatement
at any time after the effective date of revocation of authority.
The application must:
1.   Recite the name of the foreign limited liability company
and the effective date of its revocation of authority;
2.   State that the ground or grounds for revocation of authority either did not exist or have been eliminated and that no
further grounds currently exist for revocation of authority;
3.   State that the foreign limited liability company's name
satisfies the requirements of s. 608.506; and
4.   State that all taxes, fees, and penalties owed by the limited liability company and computed at the rate provided by
law at the time the foreign limited liability company applies
for reinstatement have been paid; or
(b)   As an alternative, the foreign limited liability company
may submit a current annual report, signed by the registered
agent and a manager or managing member, which substantially complies with the requirements of paragraph (a).
(2)   If the Department of State determines that the application contains the information required by subsection (1) and
that the information is correct, it shall cancel the certificate of
revocation of authority.
(3)   When the reinstatement is effective, it relates back to
and takes effect as of the effective date of the revocation of
authority, and the foreign limited liability company resumes
carrying on its business as if the revocation of authority had
never occurred.
(4)   The name of the foreign limited liability company the
certificate of authority of which has been revoked is not available for assumption or use by another limited liability
company until 1 year after the effective date of revocation of
authority unless the limited liability company provides the
Department of State with an affidavit executed as required by
s. 608.408 permitting the immediate assumption or use of its
name by another limited liability company.
(5)   If the name of the foreign limited liability company has
been lawfully assumed in this state by another limited liability company, the Department of State shall require the foreign
limited liability company to comply with s. 608.506 before
accepting its application for reinstatement.
History.—
s. 72, ch. 93-284; s. 1, ch. 99-315.

608.514 Appeal from revocation.—
(1)   If the Department of State revokes the authority of any
foreign limited liability company to transact business in this
state pursuant to the provisions of this chapter, such foreign
limited liability company may likewise appeal to the circuit
court of the county where the registered office of such limited
liability company in this state is situated by filing with the
clerk of such court a petition setting forth a copy of its application for authority to transact business in this state and a
copy of the certificate of revocation given by the Department
of State, whereupon the matter shall be tried de novo by the
court, and the court shall either sustain the action of the
Department of State or direct the department to take such
action as the court deems proper.
(2)   Appeals from all final orders and judgments entered by
the circuit court under this section in review of any ruling or
decision of the Department of State may be taken as in other
civil actions.

History.—
s. 73, ch. 93-284.

608.601 Member's derivative actions.—
(1)   A person may not commence a proceeding in the right of
a domestic or foreign limited liability company unless the
person was a member of the limited liability company when
the transaction complained of occurred or unless the person
became a member through transfer by operation of law from
one who was a member at that time.
(2)   A complaint in a proceeding brought in the right of a
limited liability company must be verified and allege with
particularity the demand made to obtain action by the managing members of a member-managed company or the managers
of a manager-managed company and that the demand was
refused or ignored. If the limited liability company com-
mences an investigation of the charges made in the demand or
complaint, the court may stay any proceeding until the investigation is completed.
(3)   The court may dismiss a derivative proceeding if, on
motion by the limited liability company, the court finds that
one of the groups specified in paragraphs (a)-(c) has made a
determination in good faith after conducting a reasonable
investigation upon which its conclusions are based that the
maintenance of the derivative suit is not in the best interests
of the limited liability company. The limited liability company shall have the burden of proving the independence and
good faith of the group making the determination and the rea-
sonableness of the investigation. The determination shall be
made by:
(a)   A majority vote of independent managing members of a
member-managed company or of independent managers of a
manager-managed company present at a meeting of the managing members of a member-managed company or of managers
of a manager-managed company, if the independent managing
members or managers, as applicable, constitute a quorum;
(b)   A majority vote of a committee consisting of two or
more independent managing members of a member-managed
company or of independent managers of a manager-managed
company appointed by a majority vote of independent managing members or managers, as applicable, present at a meeting
of the managing members of a member-managed company or
of managers of a manager-managed company, whether or not
such independent managing members or managers, as applicable, constitute a quorum; or
(c)   A panel of one or more independent persons appointed
by the court upon motion by the limited liability company.
(4)   A proceeding commenced under this section may not be
discontinued or settled without the court's approval. If the
court determines that a proposed discontinuance or settlement
will substantially affect the interest of the limited liability
company's members or a class, series, or voting group of
members, the court shall direct that notice be given to the
members affected. The court may determine which party or
parties to the proceeding shall bear the expense of giving the
notice.
(5)   On termination of the proceeding, the court may require
the plaintiff to pay any defendant's reasonable expenses,
including reasonable attorney's fees, incurred in defending
the proceeding if it finds that the proceeding was commenced
without reasonable cause.
(6)   The court may award reasonable expenses for maintaining the proceeding, including reasonable attorney's fees, to a
successful plaintiff or to the person commencing the proceeding who receives any relief, whether by judgment,
compromise, or settlement, and require that the person account
for the remainder of any proceeds to the limited liability company; however, this subsection does not apply to any relief
rendered for the benefit of injured members only and limited
to a recovery of the loss or damage of the injured members.

(7)   For purposes of this section, "member" includes a beneficial owner whose limited liability company interests are held in a voting trust or held by a nominee on the member's behalf.
History.—
s. 1, ch. 99-315.

608.701   Application of corporation case law to set aside limited liability.—
In any case in which a party seeks to hold the members of a limited liability company personally responsible for the liabilities or alleged improper actions of the limited liability company, the court shall apply the case law which interprets the conditions and circumstances under which the corporate veil of a corporation may be pierced under the law of this state.
History.—
s. 1, ch. 99-315.

608.702   Certificates and certified copies to be received in evidence.—
All certificates issued by the Department of State in accordance with this chapter, and all copies of records filed in the Department of State in accordance with this chapter when certified by the Department of State, shall be taken and received in all courts, public offices, and official bodies as prima facie evidence of the facts therein stated. A certificate under the seal of the Department of State, as to the existence or nonexistence of the facts relating to a limited liability company or foreign limited liability company, shall be taken and received in all courts, public offices, and official bodies as prima facie evidence of the existence or nonexistence of the facts therein stated.
History.—
s. 1, ch. 99-315.

608.703   Interrogatories by Department of State.—
(1)   The Department of State may direct to any limited liability company or foreign limited liability company subject to this chapter, and to any member or manager of any limited liability company or foreign limited liability company subject to this chapter, any interrogatories reasonably necessary and proper to enable the Department of State to ascertain whether the limited liability company or foreign limited liability company has complied with all of the provisions of this chapter applicable to the limited liability company or foreign limited liability company. The interrogatories shall be answered within 30 days after the date of mailing, or within such additional time as fixed by the Department of State. The answers to the interrogatories shall be full and complete and shall be made in writing and under oath. If the interrogatories are directed to an individual, they shall be answered by the individual, and if directed to a limited liability company or foreign limited liability company, they shall be answered by a manager of a manager-managed company, a member of a member-managed company, or a fiduciary if the company is in the hands of a receiver, trustee, or other court-appointed fiduciary.
(2)   The Department of State need not file any record in a court of competent jurisdiction to which the interrogatories relate until the interrogatories are answered as provided in this chapter, and not then if the answers thereto disclose that the record is not in conformity with the requirements of this chapter or if the Department of State has determined that the parties to such document have not paid all fees, taxes, and penalties due and owing this state. The Department of State shall certify to the Department of Legal Affairs, for such action as the Department of Legal Affairs may deem appropriate, all interrogatories and answers which disclose a violation of this chapter.
(3)   The Department of State may, based upon its findings hereunder or as provided in s. 213.053(15), bring an action in circuit court to collect any penalties, fees, or taxes determined to be due and owing the state and to compel any filing, qualification, or registration required by law. In connection with such proceeding, the department may, without prior approval by the court, file a lis pendens against any property owned by the corporation and may further certify any findings to the Department of Legal Affairs for the initiation of any action permitted pursuant to this chapter which the Department of Legal Affairs may deem appropriate.
(4)   The Department of State shall have the power and authority reasonably necessary to enable it to administer this chapter efficiently, to perform the duties herein imposed upon it, and to adopt reasonable rules necessary to carry out its duties and functions under this chapter.
History.—
s. 1, ch. 99-315; s. 6, ch. 2006-85.

608.704   Reservation of power to amend or repeal.—
The Legislature has the power to amend or repeal all or part of this chapter at any time, and all domestic and foreign limited liability companies subject to this chapter shall be governed by the amendment or repeal.
History.—
s. 32, ch. 2002-272.

608.705   Effect of repeal of prior acts.—
(1)   Except as provided in subsection (2), the repeal of a statute by this chapter does not affect:
(a)   The operation of the statute or any action taken under it before its repeal, including, without limiting the generality of the foregoing, the continuing validity of any provision of the articles of organization, regulations, or operating agreements of a limited liability company authorized by the statute at the time of its adoption;
(b)   Any ratification, right, remedy, privilege, obligation, or liability acquired, accrued, or incurred under the statute before its repeal;
(c)   Any violation of the statute, or any penalty, forfeiture, or punishment incurred because of the violation, before its repeal;
(d)   Any proceeding, merger, sale of assets, reorganization, or dissolution commenced under the statute before its repeal, and the proceeding, merger, sale of assets, reorganization, or dissolution may be completed in accordance with the statute as if it had not been repealed.
(2)   If a penalty or punishment imposed for violation of a statute is reduced by this chapter, the penalty or punishment if not already imposed shall be imposed in accordance with this chapter.
History.—s. 33, ch. 2002-272.

Appendix B: Checklist for Forming a Florida LLC

The checklist on the following page will help you to organize your start-up procedures. (Refer to the text of the chapters if you have any questions on the items appearing here.)

CHECKLIST FOR FORMING A FLORIDA LLC

☐ Decide on a company name.

☐ Search the name to be sure it is not already taken.

☐ Prepare and file **ARTICLES OF ORGANIZATION**.

☐ Obtain Federal Employer Identification Number (IRS Form SS-4).

☐ Prepare **ENTITY CLASSIFICATION ELECTION** (IRS Form 8832) choosing tax status (file within seventy-five days if corporate taxation).

☐ Prepare and file Form 2553 if S corporation status is desired (file within seventy-five days of formation).

☐ Decide on capitalization and tax planning.

☐ If necessary, meet with securities lawyer regarding nonparticipating members.

☐ Prepare **MEMBER-MANAGED OPERATING AGREEMENT** or **MANAGEMENT OPERATING AGREEMENT**.

☐ Hold organizational meeting.

☐ Complete **MEMBER-MANAGED OPERATING AGREEMENT** or **MANAGEMENT OPERATING AGREEMENT**.

☐ Complete **BILL OF SALE** if property is traded for interest.

☐ Open bank account.

☐ File fictitious name registration if one will be used.

☐ File trademark application if desired.

☐ Get city or county licenses, if needed.

Appendix C: Sample, Filled-In Forms

The following forms are samples of some of the forms that appear in Appendix C.

ARTICLES OF ORGANIZATION FOR FLORIDA LIMITED LIABILITY COMPANY

ARTICLE I - Name:

The name of the Limited Liability Company is:

Acme Services, LLC

ARTICLE II - Address:

The mailing address and street address of the principal office of the Limited Liability Company is:

Principal Office Address:	**Mailing Address:**
123 Main Street	123 Main Street
Anytown, FL 32100	Anytown, FL 32100

ARTICLE III - Registered Agent, Registered Office, & Registered Agent's Signature:

The name and the Florida street address of the registered agent are:

John Smith

Name

123 Main Street

Florida street address (P.O. Box **NOT** acceptable)

Anytown   FL   32100

City, State, and Zip

Having been named as registered agent and to accept service of process for the above stated limited liability company at the place designated in this certificate, I hereby accept the appointment as registered agent and agree to act in this capacity. I further agree to comply with the provisions of all statutes relating to the proper and complete performance of my duties, and I am familiar with and accept the obligations of my position as registered agent as provided for in Chapter 608, F.S..

John Smith

Registered Agent's Signature

(CONTINUED)

116

ARTICLE IV- Manager(s) or Managing Member(s):
The name and address of each Manager or Managing Member is as follows:

<u>**Title:**</u>

"MGR" = Manager
"MGRM" = Managing Member

<u>MGRM</u>

<u>**Name and Address:**</u>

John Smith
123 Main Street
Anytown, FL   32100

(Use attachment if necessary)

NOTE: An additional article must be added if an effective date is requested.

REQUIRED SIGNATURE:

John Smith
Signature of a member or an authorized representative of a member.

(In accordance with section 608.408(3), Florida Statutes, the execution
of this document constitutes an affirmation under the penalties of perjury
that the facts stated herein are true.)

John Smith
Typed or printed name of signee

<u>**Filing Fees:**</u>

**$125.00 Filing Fee for Articles of Organization and Designation
        of Registered Agent**
$ 30.00 Certified Copy (Optional)
$ 5.00 Certificate of Status (Optional)

CERTIFICATE OF CONVERSION

Pursuant to section 608.439, Florida Statutes, the following unincorporated business entity hereby submits the ***attached articles of organization*** and this certificate of conversion to convert to a Florida limited liability company:

FIRST: The name of the unincorporated business immediately prior to filing this document was:

Jones & Jones
_____.

SECOND: The date on which and the jurisdiction in which the unincorporated business was first created or otherwise came into being are:

A. Date: May 6, 2002 _____

B. Jurisdiction: Florida _____

C. If different from the above noted jurisdiction, the jurisdiction immediately prior to its conversion: _____.

THIRD: The name of the limited liability company as set forth in the ***attached*** articles of organization is:

Jones & Jones, LLC
_____.

Bob Jones
_____
Signature of a Member or an Authorized Representative of a Member
(In accordance with section 608.408(3), Florida Statutes, the execution of this document constitutes an affirmation under the penalties of perjury that the facts stated herein are true.)

Bob Jones
_____
Typed or Printed Name of Signee

FILING FEES:
$100.00 Filing Fee for Articles of Organization
$ 25.00 Filing Fee for Registered Agent Designation
$ 25.00 Filing Fee for Certificate of Conversion
$ 30.00 Certified Copy (optional)
$ 5.00 Certificate of Status (optional)

(Note: Section 608.439, F.S., does not provide for a corporation to convert to a limited liability company.)

INHS11(10/99)

This page intentionally left blank

CERTIFICATE OF MERGER

The following articles of merger are being submitted in accordance with section(s) 607.1109, 608.4382, and/or 620.203, Florida Statutes.

FIRST: The exact name, street address of its principal office, jurisdiction, and entity type for each **merging** party are as follows:

Name and Street Address	Jurisdiction	Entity Type
1. Jones & Jones 123 Main Street	Florida	Partnership

Florida Document/Registration Number: 123987456   FEI Number: 59-12345678

2. Smith & Smith 127 Main Street Anytown, FL 32100	Florida	Partnership

Florida Document/Registration Number: 987654321   FEI Number: 59-87654321

3. _____   _____   _____

_____

_____

Florida Document/Registration Number:_____   FEI Number:_____

4. _____   _____   _____

_____

_____

Florida Document/Registration Number:_____   FEI Number:_____

(Attach additional sheet(s) if necessary)

CR2E080(9/00)

SECOND: The exact name, street address of its principal office, jurisdiction, and entity type of the **surviving** party are as follows:

Name and Street Address	Jurisdiction	Entity Type
Jones & Smith, LLC	Florida	LLC
123 Main Street		
Anytown, FL 32100		

Florida Document/Registration Number: 543219876   FEI Number: 59-543987654

THIRD: The attached Plan of Merger meets the requirements of section(s) 607.1108, 608.438, 617.1103, and/or 620.201, Florida Statutes, and was approved by each domestic corporation, limited liability company, partnership and/or limited partnership that is a party to the merger in accordance with Chapter(s) 607, 617, 608, and/or 620, Florida Statutes.

FOURTH: If applicable, the attached Plan of Merger was approved by the other business entity(ies) that is/are party(ies) to the merger in accordance with the respective laws of all applicable jurisdictions.

FIFTH: If not incorporated, organized, or otherwise formed under the laws of the state of Florida, the surviving entity hereby appoints the Florida Secretary of State as its agent for substitute service of process pursuant to Chapter 48, Florida Statutes, in any proceeding to enforce any obligation or rights of any dissenting shareholders, partners, and/or members of each domestic corporation, partnership, limited partnership and/or limited liability company that is a party to the merger.

SIXTH: If not incorporated, organized, or otherwise formed under the laws of the state of Florida, the surviving entity agrees to pay the dissenting shareholders, partners, and/or members of each domestic corporation, partnership, limited partnership and/or limited liability company that is a party to the merger the amount, if any, to which they are entitled under section(s) 607.1302, 620.205, and/or 608.4384, Florida Statutes.

SEVENTH: If applicable, the surviving entity has obtained the written consent of each shareholder, member or person that as a result of the merger is now a general partner of the surviving entity pursuant to section(s) 607.1108(5), 608.4381(2), and/or 620.202(2), Florida Statutes.

EIGHTH: The merger is permitted under the respective laws of all applicable jurisdictions and is not prohibited by the agreement of any partnership or limited partnership or the regulations or articles of organization of any limited liability company that is a party to the merger.

NINTH: The merger shall become effective as of:

The date the Articles of Merger are filed with Florida Department of State

OR

January 29, 2005

(Enter specific date. NOTE: Date cannot be prior to the date of filing.)

TENTH: The Articles of Merger comply and were executed in accordance with the laws of each party's applicable jurisdiction.

ELEVENTH: SIGNATURE(S) FOR EACH PARTY:

(Note: Please see instructions for required signatures.)

Name of Entity	Signature(s)	Typed or Printed Name of Individual
Jones & Jones	*Bob Jones*	Bob Jones
	Betty Jones	Betty Jones
Smith & Smith	*Winston B. Smith*	Winston B. Smith
	Harold Jenkins Smith	Harold Jenkins Smith

(Attach additional sheet(s) if necessary)

REQUIRED SIGNATURES FOR EACH ENTITY TYPE:

All Corporations: Signature of Chairman, Vice Chairman, President or any officer.

All General Partnerships: Signatures of two partners.

All Domestic Limited Partnerships: Signatures of all general partners.

All Non-Florida Limited Partnerships: Signature of one general partner.

All Limited Liability Companies: Signature of a member or authorized representative of a member.

All Other Business Entities: In accordance with the laws of their jurisdiction.

Make checks payable to Florida Department of State and mail to:

Mailing address: Street Address:
Division of Corporations   Division of Corporations
P.O. Box 6327   409 E. Gaines St.
Tallahassee, FL 32314   Tallahassee, FL 32399

FILING FEES:

For each Limited Partnership:	$52.50 (If merger filed pursuant to s. 608.4382, $25.00)
For each Limited Liability Company:	$25.00
For each Corporation:	$35.00
For each General Partnership	$25.00
All Others:	No Charge

PLAN OF MERGER

The following plan of merger, which was adopted and approved by each party to the merger in accordance with section(s) 607.1107, 617.1103, 608.4381, and/or 620.202, is being submitted in accordance with section(s) 607.1108, 608.438, and/or 620.201, Florida Statutes.

FIRST: The exact name and jurisdiction of each **merging** party are as follows:

Name   Jurisdiction

   Jones & Jones   Florida

   Smith & Smith   Florida

SECOND: The exact name and jurisdiction of the **surviving** party are as follows:

Name   Jurisdiction

   Jones & Smith, LLC   Florida

THIRD: The terms and conditions of the merger are as follows:

Each partnership will pay off its existing liabilities and contribute all of its assets to the new LLC. Each 50% partner will become an owner of a 25% membership interest in the new LLC.

(Attach additional sheet(s) if necessary)

FOURTH:

A. The manner and basis of converting the interests, shares, obligations or other securities of each merged party into the interests, shares, obligations or other securities of the survivor, in whole or in part, into cash or other property are as follows:

Each partner's 50% interest in the partnerships will be converted into a 25% interest in the LLC.

B. The manner and basis of converting <u>rights to acquire</u> interests, shares, obligations or other securities of each merged party into <u>rights to acquire</u> interests, shares, obligations or other securities of the surviving entity, in whole or in part, into cash or other property are as follows:

There are no rights to acquire outstanding.

(Attach additional sheet(s) if necessary)

FIFTH: If a partnership or limited partnership is the surviving entity, the name(s) and address(es) of the general partner(s) are as follows:

	If General Partner is a Non-Individual,
<u>Name(s) and Address(es) of General Partner(s)</u>	<u>Florida Document/Registration Number</u>

The surviving entity is not a general partnership.

SIXTH: If a limited liability company is the surviving entity and it is to be managed by one or more managers, the name(s) and address(es) of the manager(s) are as follows:

The surviving entity is a limited liability company that will be managed by its members.

SEVENTH: All statements that are required by the laws of the jurisdiction(s) under which each Non-Florida business entity that is a party to the merger is formed, organized, or incorporated are as follows:

All entities are Florida entities.

EIGHTH: Other provisions, if any, relating to the merger:

None

(Attach additional sheet(s) if necessary)

This page intentionally left blank

Form **SS-4**

(Rev. February 2006)

Department of the Treasury
Internal Revenue Service

Application for Employer Identification Number

(For use by employers, corporations, partnerships, trusts, estates, churches, government agencies, Indian tribal entities, certain individuals, and others.)

▶ **See separate instructions for each line.**   ▶ **Keep a copy for your records.**

OMB No. 1545-0003

EIN

Type or print clearly.

1 Legal name of entity (or individual) for whom the EIN is being requested
Doe Company LLC

2 Trade name of business (if different from name on line 1)

3 Executor, administrator, trustee, "care of" name

4a Mailing address (room, apt., suite no. and street, or P.O. box)
123 Main Street

5a Street address (if different) (Do not enter a P.O. box.)

4b City, state, and ZIP code
Libertyville, FL 33461

5b City, state, and ZIP code

6 County and state where principal business is located
Libertyville, FL

7a Name of principal officer, general partner, grantor, owner, or trustor
John Doe

7b SSN, ITIN, or EIN
123-45-6789

8a **Type of entity** (check only one box)

☐ Sole proprietor (SSN) _____
☐ Partnership
☐ Corporation (enter form number to be filed) ▶ _____
☐ Personal service corporation
☐ Church or church-controlled organization
☐ Other nonprofit organization (specify) ▶ _____
☒ Other (specify) ▶ Multi-member LLC

☐ Estate (SSN of decedent) _____
☐ Plan administrator (SSN) _____
☐ Trust (SSN of grantor) _____
☐ National Guard   ☐ State/local government
☐ Farmers' cooperative   ☐ Federal government/military
☐ REMIC   ☐ Indian tribal governments/enterprises
Group Exemption Number (GEN) ▶ _____

8b If a corporation, name the state or foreign country (if applicable) where incorporated

State

Foreign country

9 **Reason for applying** (check only one box)

☒ Started new business (specify type) ▶ _____
clothing manufacturer

☐ Hired employees (Check the box and see line 12.)
☐ Compliance with IRS withholding regulations
☐ Other (specify) ▶

☐ Banking purpose (specify purpose) ▶ _____
☐ Changed type of organization (specify new type) ▶ _____
☐ Purchased going business
☐ Created a trust (specify type) ▶ _____
☐ Created a pension plan (specify type) ▶ _____

10 Date business started or acquired (month, day, year). See instructions.
10-15-2004

11 Closing month of accounting year
December

12 First date wages or annuities were paid (month, day, year). **Note.** If applicant is a withholding agent, enter date income will first be paid to nonresident alien. (month, day, year) . . . . ▶ 10-22-2004

13 Highest number of employees expected in the next 12 months (enter -0- if none).

Do you expect to have $1,000 or less in employment tax liability for the calendar year? ☐ **Yes** ☐ **No.** (If you expect to pay $4,000 or less in wages, you can mark yes.)

Agricultural	Household	Other

14 Check **one** box that best describes the principal activity of your business. ☐ Health care & social assistance ☒ Wholesale–agent/broker

☐ Construction ☒ Rental & leasing ☐ Transportation & warehousing ☐ Accommodation & food service ☐ Wholesale–other ☐ Retail
☐ Real estate ☐ Manufacturing ☐ Finance & insurance ☐ Other (specify)

15 Indicate principal line of merchandise sold, specific construction work done, products produced, or services provided.
clothing

16a Has the applicant ever applied for an employer identification number for this or any other business? . . . . ☐ **Yes** ☒ **No**
Note. If "Yes," please complete lines 16b and 16c.

16b If you checked "Yes" on line 16a, give applicant's legal name and trade name shown on prior application if different from line 1 or 2 above.
Legal name ▶   Trade name ▶

16c Approximate date when, and city and state where, the application was filed. Enter previous employer identification number if known.

Approximate date when filed (mo., day, year)	City and state where filed	Previous EIN

Third Party Designee

Complete this section **only** if you want to authorize the named individual to receive the entity's EIN and answer questions about the completion of this form.

Designee's name

Address and ZIP code

Designee's telephone number (include area code)
(   )

Designee's fax number (include area code)
(   )

Under penalties of perjury, I declare that I have examined this application, and to the best of my knowledge and belief, it is true, correct, and complete.

Name and title (type or print clearly) ▶ John Doe, Member

Signature ▶ *John Doe*   Date ▶ 10/15/04

Applicant's telephone number (include area code)
(518) 555-0000

Applicant's fax number (include area code)
(   )

For Privacy Act and Paperwork Reduction Act Notice, see separate instructions.   Cat. No. 16055N   Form **SS-4** (Rev. 2-2006)

This page intentionally left blank

Bill of Sale

The undersigned, in consideration of the receipt of <u>100</u> % of the membership interest in <u>Acme Services, LLC</u>, a Florida limited liability company, hereby grants, bargains, sells, transfers, and delivers unto said company the following goods and chattels:

2 desks

3 chairs

2 telephones

3 filing cabinets

1 bookcase

1 copier

2 computers

1 answering machine

To have and to hold the same forever.

And the undersigned, their heirs, successors, and administrators, covenant and warrant that they are the lawful owners of the said goods and chattels and that they are free from all encumbrances. That the undersigned have the right to sell this property and that they will warrant and defend the sale of said property against the lawful claims and demands of all persons.

IN WITNESS whereof the undersigned have executed this Bill of Sale this <u>15</u> day of <u>June</u>, <u>2005</u>.

John Smith
_____

This page intentionally left blank

Schedule A to
Limited Liability Company
Operating or Management Agreement of
Acme Services, LLC

1. **Initial member(s):** The initial member(s) are:

   John Smith

2. **Capital Contribution(s):** The capital contribution(s) of the member(s) is/are:

   All of the assets of Smith Enterprises as listed on Bill of Sale plus $3,500 in cash

3. **Profits and Losses:** The profits, losses and other tax matters shall be allocated among the members in the following percentages:

   John Smith 100%

4. **Management:** The company shall be managed by:

   The member, John Smith

5. **Registered Agent:** the initial registered agent and registered office of the company are:

   John Smith, 123 Main Street, Anytown, Florida 32100

6. **Tax Matters:** The tax matters partner is:

   John Smith

This page intentionally left blank

Minutes of a Meeting of Members of

Acme Services, LLC

A meeting of the members of the company was held on June 20, 2005 , at 123 Main Street, Anytown, Florida 32100 .

The following were present, being all the members of the limited liability company:
John Smith

The meeting was called to order and it was moved, seconded and unanimously carried that John Smith act as Chairman and that John Smith act as Secretary.

After discussion and upon motion duly made, seconded and carried the following resolution(s) were adopted:

This company will borrow $20,000 and purchase a 2004 Ford F150 truck from Anytown Motors.

There being no further business to come before the meeting, upon motion duly made, seconded and unanimously carried, it was adjourned.

John Smith
Secretary

Members:

This page intentionally left blank

Certificate of Authority

for

Acme Services, LLC

This is to certify that the above limited liability company is managed by its

☒ members

☐ managers

who are listed below and that each of them is authorized and empowered to transact business on behalf of the company.

Name	Address
John Smith	123 Main Street
	Anytown, FL 32100

Date: _____August 9, 2005_____

Name of company:

Acme Services, LLC

By: _____*John Smith*_____

Position: _Member_

This page intentionally left blank

Banking Resolution of

Acme Services, LLC

The undersigned, being a member of the above limited liability company authorized to sign this resolution, hereby certifies that on the __3__ day of _____January_____, __2005__ the members of the limited liability company adopted the following resolution:

RESOLVED that the limited liability company open bank accounts with _____Anytown National Bank_____ and that the members of the company are authorized to take such action as is necessary to open such accounts; that the bank's printed form of resolution is hereby adopted and incorporated into these minutes by reference; that any __1__ of the following person(s) shall have signature authority over the account:

_____John Smith_____   _____

_____   _____

and that said resolution has not been modified or rescinded.

Date: _____January 3, 2005_____

_____*John Smith*_____
Authorized member

This page intentionally left blank

Appendix D:
Blank Forms

This appendix contains the forms referred to in the various sections of this book. To use them, you should first tear them out and make photocopies of the ones you will need.

This page intentionally left blank

TRANSMITTAL LETTER

TO: Registration Section
Division of Corporations

SUBJECT: _____
(Name of Limited Liability Company)

The enclosed Articles of Organization and fee(s) are submitted for filing.

Please return all correspondence concerning this matter to the following:

_____
(Name of Person)

_____
(Firm/Company)

_____
(Address)

_____
(City/State and Zip Code)

For further information concerning this matter, please call:

_____ at (_____) _____
(Name of Person)   (Area Code & Daytime Telephone Number)

Enclosed is a check for the following amount:

❒ $125.00 Filing Fee   ❒ $130.00 Filing Fee &   ❒ $155.00 Filing Fee &   ❒ $160.00 Filing Fee,
Certificate of Status   Certified Copy   Certificate of Status &
(additional copy is enclosed)   Certified Copy
(additional copy is enclosed)

STREET ADDRESS:
Registration Section
Division of Corporations
409 E. Gaines Street
Tallahassee, Florida 32399

MAILING ADDRESS:
Registration Section
Division of Corporations
P.O. Box 6327
Tallahassee, Florida 32314

This page intentionally left blank

FLORIDA DEPARTMENT OF STATE
DIVISION OF CORPORATIONS

Attached are the forms and instructions to form a Florida Limited Liability Company pursuant to Chapter 608, Florida Statutes. All information included in the Articles of Organization must be in English and must be typewritten or printed legibly. If this requirement is not met, the document will be returned for correction(s). The Division of Corporations suggests using the sample articles merely as a guideline. Pursuant to s. 608.407, Florida Statutes, additional information may be contained in the Articles of Organization.

Pursuant to section 608.406(2), the name of the limited liability company shall be filed with the Department of State for public notice only and shall not alone create any presumption of ownership beyond that which is created under the common law. The Department of State shall record the name without regard to any other name recorded.

NOTE: This form for filing Articles of Organization is basic. Each limited liability company is a separate entity and as such has specific goals, needs, and requirements. Additionally, the tax consequences arising from the structure of a limited liability company can be significant. The Division of Corporations recommends that all documents be reviewed by your legal counsel. The Division is a filing agency and as such does not render any legal, accounting, or tax advice. The professional advice of your legal counsel to ascertain exact compliance with all statutory requirements is strongly recommended.

Pursuant to s. 608.407, Florida Statutes, the Articles of Organization must set forth the following:

ARTICLE I:

The name of the limited liability company, which **must** end with the words "limited liability company" or "limited company" or their abbreviation "L.L.C.", "L.C.", "LLC" or "LC". (The word "limited" may be abbreviated as "Ltd." and the word "company" may be abbreviated as "Co".)

ARTICLE II:
The mailing address and the street address of the principal office of the limited liability company.

ARTICLE III:
The name and Florida street address of the limited liability company's registered agent. The registered agent must sign and state that he/she is familiar with and accepts the obligations of the position.

ARTICLE IV: The name and address of each Manager or Managing member. Insert "MGR" for each Manager. Insert "MGRM" for each Managing Member. **IMPORTANT: Most financial institutions require this information to be recorded with the Florida Department of State.**

CR2E047 (8/05)

ARTICLE V: If an effective date is listed, the date must be specific and cannot be more than five business days prior to or 90 days after the date of filing.

Articles of Organization must be executed by at least one member or authorized representative of a member, and the execution of the document constitutes an affirmation under the penalties of perjury that the facts stated therein are true.

FILING FEES:

$ 125.00 Filing Fee for Articles of Organization and Designation of Registered Agent
$ 30.00 Certified Copy (OPTIONAL)
$ 5.00 Certificate of Status (OPTIONAL)

A letter of acknowledgment will be issued free of charge upon registration. Please submit one check made payable to the Florida Department of State for the total amount of the filing fees and any optional certificate or copy.

A cover letter containing your name, address and daytime telephone number should be submitted along with the articles of organization and the check. The mailing address and courier address are:

Mailing Address	**Street/Courier Address**
Registration Section	Registration Section
Division of Corporations	Division of Corporations
P.O. Box 6327	Clifton Building
Tallahassee, FL 32314	2661 Executive Center Circle
(850) 245-6051	Tallahassee, FL 32301
	(850) 245-6051

Any further inquiries concerning this matter should be directed to the Registration Section by calling (850) 245-6051.

ARTICLES OF ORGANIZATION FOR FLORIDA LIMITED LIABILITY COMPANY

ARTICLE I - Name:

The name of the Limited Liability Company is:

_____

(Must end with the words "Limited Liability Company, "Limited Company" or their abbreviation "LLC," or "L.C.,")

ARTICLE II - Address:

The mailing address and street address of the principal office of the Limited Liability Company is:

Principal Office Address: **Mailing Address:**

_____   _____

_____   _____

_____   _____

ARTICLE III - Registered Agent, Registered Office, & Registered Agent's Signature:

(The Limited Liability Company cannot serve as its own Registered Agent. You must designate an individual or another business entity with an active Florida registration.)

The name and the Florida street address of the registered agent are:

_____

Name

_____

Florida street address (P.O. Box **NOT** acceptable)

_____ FL _____

City, State, and Zip

Having been named as registered agent and to accept service of process for the above stated limited liability company at the place designated in this certificate, I hereby accept the appointment as registered agent and agree to act in this capacity. I further agree to comply with the provisions of all statutes relating to the proper and complete performance of my duties, and I am familiar with and accept the obligations of my position as registered agent as provided for in Chapter 608, F.S..

_____

Registered Agent's Signature (REQUIRED)

(CONTINUED)
Page 1 of 2

ARTICLE IV- Manager(s) or Managing Member(s):

The name and address of each Manager or Managing Member is as follows:

Title: **Name and Address:**

"MGR" = Manager

"MGRM" = Managing Member

_____   _____
                                   _____
                                   _____

_____   _____
                                   _____
                                   _____

_____   _____
                                   _____
                                   _____

_____   _____
                                   _____
                                   _____

(Use attachment if necessary)

ARTICLE V: Effective date, if other than the date of filing: _____. (OPTIONAL)
(If an effective date is listed, the date must be specific and cannot be more than five business days prior to or 90 days after the date of filing.)

REQUIRED SIGNATURE:

_____
Signature of a member or an authorized representative of a member.

(In accordance with section 608.408(3), Florida Statutes, the execution
of this document constitutes an affirmation under the penalties of perjury
that the facts stated herein are true.)

_____
Typed or printed name of signee

Filing Fees:

**$125.00 Filing Fee for Articles of Organization and Designation
        of Registered Agent**
$ 30.00 Certified Copy (Optional)
$ 5.00 Certificate of Status (Optional)

Page 2 of 2

ARTICLES OF ORGANIZATION FOR FLORIDA
PROFESSIONAL LIMITED LIABILITY COMPANY

ARTICLE I - Name:

The name of the Limited Liability Company is:

ARTICLE II - Address:

The mailing address and street address of the principal office of the Limited Liability Company is:

ARTICLE III - Registered Agent

The name and street address of the initial registered agent are:

ARTICLE IV - Management:

(Check the appropriate box)

☐ The Limited Liability Company is to be a manager-managed company.
☐ The Limited Liability Company is to be managed by the members.

ARTICLE V - Professional Limited Liability Company

This limited liability company shall be a professional limited liability company under Florida statutes chapter 621. The business of the company is limited to the one profession of _____ _____ and no person or entity shall be admitted as member unless he, she or it is qualified to practice this profession. Further, no interest can be sold except to someone so qualified.

_____

Signature of a member or an authorized representative of a member.

(In accordance with section 608.408(3), Florida Statutes, the execution of this affidavit constitutes an affirmation under the penalties of perjury that the facts stated herein are true.)

_____

Typed or printed name of signee

Filing Fee: $100.00 for Articles

This page intentionally left blank

Certificate of Conversion
For
"Other Business Entity"
Into
Florida Limited Liability Company

This Certificate of Conversion **and attached Articles of Organization** are submitted to convert the following **"Other Business Entity" into a Florida Limited Liability Company** in accordance with s.608.439, Florida Statutes.

1. The name of the "Other Business Entity" immediately prior to the filing of this Certificate of Conversion

(Enter Name of Other Business Entity)

2. The "Other Business Entity" is a _____
   (Enter entity type. Example: corporation, limited partnership, sole proprietorship, general partnership, common law or business trust, etc.)

first organized, formed or incorporated under the laws of _____
   (Enter state, or if a non-U.S. entity, the name of the country)

on _____
   (Enter date "Other Business Entity" was first organized, formed or incorporated)

3. If the jurisdiction of the "Other Business Entity" was changed, the state or country under the laws of which it is now organized, formed or incorporated:

_____

4. The name of the Florida Limited Liability Company as set forth in the **attached Articles of Organization:**

_____
(Enter Name of Florida Limited Liability Company)

Page 1 of 2

5. If not effective on the date of filing, enter the effective date:_____.
(The effective date: 1) cannot be prior to nor more than 90 days after the date this document is filed by the Florida Department of State; <u>AND</u> 2) must be the same as the effective date listed in the attached Articles of Organization, if an effective date is listed therein.)

Signed this _____ day of _____ 20_____.

Signature of Authorized Person:_____

Printed Name: _____ Title: _____

Fees:

Certificate of Conversion:	$25.00
Fees for Florida Articles of Organization:	$125.00
Certified Copy:	$30.00 (Optional)
Certificate of Status:	$5.00 (Optional)

Page 2 of 2

FLORIDA DEPARTMENT OF STATE
DIVISION OF CORPORATIONS

Attached is a form to file a Certificate of Merger pursuant to section 608.4382, Florida Statutes. This form is basic and may not meet all merger needs. The advice of an attorney is recommended.

Filing Fees:

$25.00 for each Limited Liability Company
$35.00 for each Corporation
$52.50 for each Limited Partnership or
    Limited Liability Limited Partnership
$25.00 for each General Partnership or Limited
    Liability Partnership
$25.00 for each Other Business Entity

Certified Copy (optional):   **$30.00**

Send one check in the total amount payable to the Florida Department of State.

Please include a cover letter containing your telephone number, return address and certification requirements, or complete the attached cover letter.

Mailing Address   **Street Address**

Registration Section   Registration Section
Division of Corporations   Division of Corporations
P. O. Box 6327   Clifton Building
Tallahassee, FL 32314   2661 Executive Center Circle
                                   Tallahassee, FL 32301

For further information, you may contact the Registration Section at (850) 245-6051.

CR2E080 (01/06)

Certificate of Merger
For
Florida Limited Liability Company

The following Certificate of Merger is submitted to merge the following Florida Limited Liability Company(ies) in accordance with s. 608.4382, Florida Statutes.

FIRST: The exact name, form/entity type, and jurisdiction for each **merging** party are as follows:

Name	Jurisdiction	Form/Entity Type
_____	_____	_____
_____	_____	_____
_____	_____	_____
_____	_____	_____

SECOND: The exact name, form/entity type, and jurisdiction of the **surviving** party are as follows:

Name	Jurisdiction	Form/Entity Type
_____	_____	_____

THIRD: The attached plan of merger was approved by each domestic corporation, limited liability company, partnership and/or limited partnership that is a party to the merger in accordance with the applicable provisions of Chapters 607, 608, 617, and/or 620, Florida Statutes.

FOURTH: The attached plan of merger was approved by each other business entity that is a party to the merger in accordance with the applicable laws of the state, country or jurisdiction under which such other business entity is formed, organized or incorporated.

FIFTH: If other than the date of filing, the effective date of the merger, which cannot be prior to nor more than 90 days after the date this document is filed by the Florida Department of State:

_____.

SIXTH: If the surviving party is not formed, organized or incorporated under the laws of Florida, the survivor's principal office address in its home state, country or jurisdiction is as follows:

_____

_____

_____

SEVENTH: If the survivor is not formed, organized or incorporated under the laws of Florida, the survivor agrees to pay to any members with appraisal rights the amount, to which such members are entitles under ss.608.4351-608.43595, F.S.

EIGHTH: If the surviving party is an out-of-state entity not qualified to transact business in this state, the surviving entity:

a.) Lists the following street and mailing address of an office, which the Florida Department of State may use for the purposes of s. 48.181, F.S., are as follows:

Street address: _____

_____

_____

Mailing address: _____

_____

_____

b.) Appoints the Florida Secretary of State as its agent for service of process in a proceeding to enforce obligations of each limited liability company that merged into such entity, including any appraisal rights of its members under ss.608.4351-608.43595, Florida Statutes.

NINTH: Signature(s) for Each Party:

Name of Entity/Organization:	Signature(s):	Typed or Printed Name of Individual:
_____	_____	_____
_____	_____	_____
_____	_____	_____
_____	_____	_____

Corporations:	Chairman, Vice Chairman, President or Officer *(If no directors selected, signature of incorporator.)*
General partnerships:	Signature of a general partner or authorized person
Florida Limited Partnerships:	Signatures of all general partners
Non-Florida Limited Partnerships:	Signature of a general partner
Limited Liability Companies:	Signature of a member or authorized representative

Fees:		
	For each Limited Liability Company:	$25.00
	For each Corporation:	$35.00
	For each Limited Partnership:	$52.50
	For each General Partnership:	$25.00
	For each Other Business Entity:	$25.00

Certified Copy (optional): $30.00

3 of 6

PLAN OF MERGER

FIRST: The exact name, form/entity type, and jurisdiction for each **merging** party are as follows:

Name	Jurisdiction	Form/Entity Type
_____	_____	_____
_____	_____	_____
_____	_____	_____
_____	_____	_____

SECOND: The exact name, form/entity type, and jurisdiction of the **surviving** party are as follows:

Name	Jurisdiction	Form/Entity Type
_____	_____	_____

THIRD: The terms and conditions of the merger are as follows:

_____

_____

_____

_____

_____

_____

_____

_____

_____

(Attach additional sheet if necessary)

4 of 6

FOURTH:

A. The manner and basis of converting the interests, shares, obligations or other securities of each merged party into the interests, shares, obligations or others securities of the survivor, in whole or in part, into cash or other property is as follows:

_____

_____

_____

_____

_____

_____

_____

(Attach additional sheet if necessary)

B. The manner and basis of converting <u>rights to acquire</u> the interests, shares, obligations or other securities of each merged party into <u>rights to acquire</u> the interests, shares, obligations or others securities of the survivor, in whole or in part, into cash or other property is as follows:

_____

_____

_____

_____

_____

_____

(Attach additional sheet if necessary)

FIFTH: Any statements that are required by the laws under which each other business entity is formed, organized, or incorporated are as follows:

_____

_____

_____

_____

_____

_____

_____

(Attach additional sheet if necessary)

SIXTH: Other provisions, if any, relating to the merger are as follows:

_____

_____

_____

_____

_____

_____

_____

(Attach additional sheet if necessary)

6 of 6

This page intentionally left blank

Form **SS-4**
(Rev. February 2006)
Department of the Treasury
Internal Revenue Service

Application for Employer Identification Number

(For use by employers, corporations, partnerships, trusts, estates, churches, government agencies, Indian tribal entities, certain individuals, and others.)

▶ See separate instructions for each line.   ▶ Keep a copy for your records.

OMB No. 1545-0003

EIN

Type or print clearly.

1 Legal name of entity (or individual) for whom the EIN is being requested

2 Trade name of business (if different from name on line 1)

3 Executor, administrator, trustee, "care of" name

4a Mailing address (room, apt., suite no. and street, or P.O. box)

5a Street address (if different) (Do not enter a P.O. box.)

4b City, state, and ZIP code

5b City, state, and ZIP code

6 County and state where principal business is located

7a Name of principal officer, general partner, grantor, owner, or trustor

7b SSN, ITIN, or EIN

8a Type of entity (check only one box)
☐ Sole proprietor (SSN) _____
☐ Partnership
☐ Corporation (enter form number to be filed) ▶ _____
☐ Personal service corporation
☐ Church or church-controlled organization
☐ Other nonprofit organization (specify) ▶ _____
☐ Other (specify) ▶
☐ Estate (SSN of decedent) _____
☐ Plan administrator (SSN) _____
☐ Trust (SSN of grantor) _____
☐ National Guard   ☐ State/local government
☐ Farmers' cooperative   ☐ Federal government/military
☐ REMIC   ☐ Indian tribal governments/enterprises
Group Exemption Number (GEN) ▶ _____

8b If a corporation, name the state or foreign country (if applicable) where incorporated
State _____   Foreign country _____

9 Reason for applying (check only one box)
☐ Started new business (specify type) ▶ _____
☐ Hired employees (Check the box and see line 12.)
☐ Compliance with IRS withholding regulations
☐ Other (specify) ▶
☐ Banking purpose (specify purpose) ▶ _____
☐ Changed type of organization (specify new type) ▶ _____
☐ Purchased going business
☐ Created a trust (specify type) ▶ _____
☐ Created a pension plan (specify type) ▶ _____

10 Date business started or acquired (month, day, year). See instructions.

11 Closing month of accounting year

12 First date wages or annuities were paid (month, day, year). **Note.** If applicant is a withholding agent, enter date income will first be paid to nonresident alien. (month, day, year) . . . . ▶

13 Highest number of employees expected in the next 12 months (enter -0- if none).
Do you expect to have $1,000 or less in employment tax liability for the calendar year? ☐ **Yes** ☐ **No.** (If you expect to pay $4,000 or less in wages, you can mark yes.)
Agricultural | Household | Other

14 Check **one** box that best describes the principal activity of your business.
☐ Construction ☐ Rental & leasing ☐ Transportation & warehousing ☐ Health care & social assistance ☐ Wholesale–agent/broker
☐ Real estate ☐ Manufacturing ☐ Finance & insurance ☐ Accommodation & food service ☐ Wholesale–other ☐ Retail
☐ Other (specify)

15 Indicate principal line of merchandise sold, specific construction work done, products produced, or services provided.

16a Has the applicant ever applied for an employer identification number for this or any other business? . . . . . ☐ **Yes** ☐ **No**
Note. If "Yes," please complete lines 16b and 16c.

16b If you checked "Yes" on line 16a, give applicant's legal name and trade name shown on prior application if different from line 1 or 2 above.
Legal name ▶   Trade name ▶

16c Approximate date when, and city and state where, the application was filed. Enter previous employer identification number if known.
Approximate date when filed (mo., day, year)   City and state where filed   Previous EIN

Third Party Designee
Complete this section **only** if you want to authorize the named individual to receive the entity's EIN and answer questions about the completion of this form.
Designee's name | Designee's telephone number (include area code) ( )
Address and ZIP code | Designee's fax number (include area code) ( )

Under penalties of perjury, I declare that I have examined this application, and to the best of my knowledge and belief, it is true, correct, and complete. | Applicant's telephone number (include area code) ( )
Name and title (type or print clearly) ▶
Signature ▶   Date ▶ | Applicant's fax number (include area code) ( )

For Privacy Act and Paperwork Reduction Act Notice, see separate instructions.   Cat. No. 16055N   Form **SS-4** (Rev. 2-2006)

Do I Need an EIN?

File Form SS-4 if the applicant entity does not already have an EIN but is required to show an EIN on any return, statement, or other document.[1] See also the separate instructions for each line on Form SS-4.

IF the applicant...	AND...	THEN...
Started a new business	Does not currently have (nor expect to have) employees	Complete lines 1, 2, 4a–8a, 8b (if applicable), and 9–16c.
Hired (or will hire) employees, including household employees	Does not already have an EIN	Complete lines 1, 2, 4a–6, 7a–b (if applicable), 8a, 8b (if applicable), and 9–16c.
Opened a bank account	Needs an EIN for banking purposes only	Complete lines 1–5b, 7a–b (if applicable), 8a, 9, and 16a–c.
Changed type of organization	Either the legal character of the organization or its ownership changed (for example, you incorporate a sole proprietorship or form a partnership)[2]	Complete lines 1–16c (as applicable).
Purchased a going business[3]	Does not already have an EIN	Complete lines 1–16c (as applicable).
Created a trust	The trust is other than a grantor trust or an IRA trust[4]	Complete lines 1–16c (as applicable).
Created a pension plan as a plan administrator[5]	Needs an EIN for reporting purposes	Complete lines 1, 3, 4a–b, 8a, 9, and 16a–c.
Is a foreign person needing an EIN to comply with IRS withholding regulations	Needs an EIN to complete a Form W-8 (other than Form W-8ECI), avoid withholding on portfolio assets, or claim tax treaty benefits[6]	Complete lines 1–5b, 7a–b (SSN or ITIN optional), 8a–9, and 16a–c.
Is administering an estate	Needs an EIN to report estate income on Form 1041	Complete lines 1, 2, 3, 4a–6, 8a, 9-11, 12-15 (if applicable), and 16a–c.
Is a withholding agent for taxes on non-wage income paid to an alien (i.e., individual, corporation, or partnership, etc.)	Is an agent, broker, fiduciary, manager, tenant, or spouse who is required to file Form 1042, Annual Withholding Tax Return for U.S. Source Income of Foreign Persons	Complete lines 1, 2, 3 (if applicable), 4a–5b, 7a–b (if applicable), 8a, 9, and 16a–c.
Is a state or local agency	Serves as a tax reporting agent for public assistance recipients under Rev. Proc. 80-4, 1980-1 C.B. 581[7]	Complete lines 1, 2, 4a–5b, 8a, 9, and 16a–c.
Is a single-member LLC	Needs an EIN to file Form 8832, Entity Classification Election, for filing employment tax returns, **or** for state reporting purposes[8]	Complete lines 1–16c (as applicable).
Is an S corporation	Needs an EIN to file Form 2553, Election by a Small Business Corporation[9]	Complete lines 1–16c (as applicable).

[1] For example, a sole proprietorship or self-employed farmer who establishes a qualified retirement plan, or is required to file excise, employment, alcohol, tobacco, or firearms returns, must have an EIN. A partnership, corporation, REMIC (real estate mortgage investment conduit), nonprofit organization (church, club, etc.), or farmers' cooperative must use an EIN for any tax-related purpose even if the entity does not have employees.

[2] However, do not apply for a new EIN if the existing entity only (a) changed its business name, (b) elected on Form 8832 to change the way it is taxed (or is covered by the default rules), or (c) terminated its partnership status because at least 50% of the total interests in partnership capital and profits were sold or exchanged within a 12-month period. The EIN of the terminated partnership should continue to be used. See Regulations section 301.6109-1(d)(2)(iii).

[3] Do not use the EIN of the prior business unless you became the "owner" of a corporation by acquiring its stock.

[4] However, grantor trusts that do not file using Optional Method 1 and IRA trusts that are required to file Form 990-T, Exempt Organization Business Income Tax Return, must have an EIN. For more information on grantor trusts, see the Instructions for Form 1041.

[5] A plan administrator is the person or group of persons specified as the administrator by the instrument under which the plan is operated.

[6] Entities applying to be a Qualified Intermediary (QI) need a QI-EIN even if they already have an EIN. See Rev. Proc. 2000-12.

[7] See also *Household employer* on page 3. **Note.** State or local agencies may need an EIN for other reasons, for example, hired employees.

[8] Most LLCs do not need to file Form 8832. See *Limited liability company (LLC)* on page 4 for details on completing Form SS-4 for an LLC.

[9] An existing corporation that is electing or revoking S corporation status should use its previously-assigned EIN.

Form **8832**
(Rev. March 2007)
Department of the Treasury
Internal Revenue Service

Entity Classification Election

OMB No. 1545-1516

Type or Print	Name of eligible entity making election	Employer identification number
	Number, street, and room or suite no. If a P.O. box, see instructions.	
	City or town, state, and ZIP code. If a foreign address, enter city, province or state, postal code and country. Follow the country's practice for entering the postal code.	

Check if: ☐ Address change

1   Type of election (see instructions):

a ☐ Initial classification by a newly-formed entity. Skip lines 2a and 2b and go to line 3.

b ☐ Change in current classification. Go to line 2a.

2a Has the eligible entity previously filed an entity election that had an effective date within the last 60 months?

☐ **Yes.** Go to line 2b.
☐ **No.** Skip line 2b and go to line 3.

2b Was the eligible entity's prior election for initial classification by a newly formed entity effective on the date of formation?

☐ **Yes.** Go to line 3.
☐ **No.** Stop here. You generally are not currently eligible to make the election (see instructions).

3 Does the eligible entity have more than one owner?

☐ **Yes.** You can elect to be classified as a partnership or an association taxable as a corporation. Skip line 4 and go to line 5.
☐ **No.** You can elect to be classified as an association taxable as a corporation or disregarded as a separate entity. Go to line 4.

4 If the eligible entity has only one owner, provide the following information:

a Name of owner ....

b Identifying number of owner ....

5 If the eligible entity is owned by one or more affiliated corporations that file a consolidated return, provide the name and employer identification number of the parent corporation:

a Name of parent corporation ....

b Employer identification number ....

For Paperwork Reduction Act Notice, see instructions.   Cat. No. 22598R   Form **8832** (Rev. 3-2007)

6 **Type of entity** (see instructions):

a ☐ A domestic eligible entity electing to be classified as an association taxable as a corporation.
b ☐ A domestic eligible entity electing to be classified as a partnership.
c ☐ A domestic eligible entity with a single owner electing to be disregarded as a separate entity.
d ☐ A foreign eligible entity electing to be classified as an association taxable as a corporation.
e ☐ A foreign eligible entity electing to be classified as a partnership.
f ☐ A foreign eligible entity with a single owner electing to be disregarded as a separate entity.

7 If the eligible entity is created or organized in a foreign jurisdiction, provide the foreign country of
organization

8 Election is to be effective beginning (month, day, year) (see instructions) . . . .   /   /

9 Name and title of contact person whom the IRS may call for more information	**10** Contact person's telephone number
	( )

Consent Statement and Signature(s) (see instructions)

Under penalties of perjury, I (we) declare that I (we) consent to the election of the above-named entity to be classified as indicated above, and that I (we) have examined this consent statement, and to the best of my (our) knowledge and belief, it is true, correct, and complete. If I am an officer, manager, or member signing for all members of the entity, I further declare that I am authorized to execute this consent statement on their behalf.

Signature(s)	Date	Title

Form **2553**
(Rev. December 2006)
Department of the Treasury
Internal Revenue Service

Election by a Small Business Corporation

(Under section 1362 of the Internal Revenue Code)
See Parts II and III on back and the separate instructions.
The corporation can fax this form to the IRS (see separate instructions).

OMB No. 1545-0146

Notes: 1. *Do not* file *Form 1120S,* U.S. Income Tax Return for an S Corporation, for any tax year before the year the election takes effect.
2. This election to be an S corporation can be accepted only if all the tests are met under **Who May Elect** on page 1 of the instructions; all shareholders have signed the consent statement; an officer has signed this form; and the exact name and address of the corporation and other required form information are provided.

Part I	Election Information

Please Type or Print

Name (see instructions)	**A** Employer identification number
Number, street, and room or suite no. (If a P.O. box, see instructions.)	**B** Date incorporated
City or town, state, and ZIP code	**C** State of incorporation

D Check the applicable box(es) if the corporation, after applying for the EIN shown in **A** above, changed its name ☐ or address ☐

E Election is to be effective for tax year beginning (month, day, year) (see instructions) . . . . / /

F Name and title of officer or legal representative who the IRS may call for more information

G Telephone number of officer or legal representative
( )

H If this election takes effect for the first tax year the corporation exists, enter month, day, and year of the **earliest** of the following: (1) date the corporation first had shareholders, (2) date the corporation first had assets, or (3) date the corporation began doing business . . . . / /

I Selected tax year: Annual return will be filed for tax year ending (month and day) ---------------------------------------

If the tax year ends on any date other than December 31, except for a 52-53-week tax year ending with reference to the month of December, complete Part II on the back. If the date you enter is the ending date of a 52-53-week tax year, write "52-53-week year" to the right of the date.

J Name and address of each shareholder or former shareholder required to consent to the election. (See the instructions for column K) If more than 100 shareholders are listed, check the box if treating members of a family as one shareholder results in no more than 100 shareholders (see test 2 under **Who May Elect** in the instructions) . . . ☐	**K** Shareholders' Consent Statement. Under penalties of perjury, we declare that we consent to the election of the above-named corporation to be an S corporation under section 1362(a) and that we have examined this consent statement, including accompanying schedules and statements, and to the best of our knowledge and belief, it is true, correct, and complete. We understand our consent is binding and may not be withdrawn after the corporation has made a valid election. (Sign and date below.)		**L** Stock owned or percentage of ownership (see instructions)		**M** Social security number or employer identification number (see instructions)	**N** Shareholder's tax year ends (month and day)
	Signature	Date	Number of shares or percentage of ownership	Date(s) acquired		

Under penalties of perjury, I declare that I have examined this election, including accompanying schedules and statements, and to the best of my knowledge and belief, it is true, correct, and complete.

Signature of officer	Title	Date

For Paperwork Reduction Act Notice, see separate instructions.   Cat. No. 18629R   Form **2553** (Rev. 12-2006)

Part II Selection of Fiscal Tax Year (see instructions)

Note: *All corporations using this part must complete item O and item P, Q, or R.*

O Check the applicable box to indicate whether the corporation is:

1. ☐ A new corporation **adopting** the tax year entered in item I, Part I.

2. ☐ An existing corporation **retaining** the tax year entered in item I, Part I.

3. ☐ An existing corporation **changing** to the tax year entered in item I, Part I.

P Complete item P if the corporation is using the automatic approval provisions of Rev. Proc. 2006-46, 2006-45 I.R.B. 859, to request **(1)** a natural business year (as defined in section 5.07 of Rev. Proc. 2006-46) or **(2)** a year that satisfies the ownership tax year test (as defined in section 5.08 of Rev. Proc. 2006-46). Check the applicable box below to indicate the representation statement the corporation is making.

1. Natural Business Year ☐ I represent that the corporation is adopting, retaining, or changing to a tax year that qualifies as its natural business year (as defined in section 5.07 of Rev. Proc. 2006-46) and has attached a statement showing separately for each month the gross receipts for the most recent 47 months (see instructions). I also represent that the corporation is not precluded by section 4.02 of Rev. Proc. 2006-46 from obtaining automatic approval of such adoption, retention, or change in tax year.

2. Ownership Tax Year ☐ I represent that shareholders (as described in section 5.08 of Rev. Proc. 2006-46) holding more than half of the shares of the stock (as of the first day of the tax year to which the request relates) of the corporation have the same tax year or are concurrently changing to the tax year that the corporation adopts, retains, or changes to per item I, Part I, and that such tax year satisfies the requirement of section 4.01(3) of Rev. Proc. 2006-46. I also represent that the corporation is not precluded by section 4.02 of Rev. Proc. 2006-46 from obtaining automatic approval of such adoption, retention, or change in tax year.

Note: *If you do not use item P and the corporation wants a fiscal tax year, complete either item Q or R below. Item Q is used to request a fiscal tax year based on a business purpose and to make a back-up section 444 election. Item R is used to make a regular section 444 election.*

Q Business Purpose—To request a fiscal tax year based on a business purpose, check box Q1. See instructions for details including payment of a user fee. You may also check box Q2 and/or box Q3.

1. Check here ☐ if the fiscal year entered in item I, Part I, is requested under the prior approval provisions of Rev. Proc. 2002-39, 2002-22 I.R.B. 1046. Attach to Form 2553 a statement describing the relevant facts and circumstances and, if applicable, the gross receipts from sales and services necessary to establish a business purpose. See the instructions for details regarding the gross receipts from sales and services. If the IRS proposes to disapprove the requested fiscal year, do you want a conference with the IRS National Office?

☐ Yes ☐ No

2. Check here ☐ to show that the corporation intends to make a back-up section 444 election in the event the corporation's business purpose request is not approved by the IRS. (See instructions for more information.)

3. Check here ☐ to show that the corporation agrees to adopt or change to a tax year ending December 31 if necessary for the IRS to accept this election for S corporation status in the event (1) the corporation's business purpose request is not approved and the corporation makes a back-up section 444 election, but is ultimately not qualified to make a section 444 election, or (2) the corporation's business purpose request is not approved and the corporation did not make a back-up section 444 election.

R Section 444 Election—To make a section 444 election, check box R1. You may also check box R2.

1. Check here ☐ to show that the corporation will make, if qualified, a section 444 election to have the fiscal tax year shown in item I, Part I. To make the election, you must complete **Form 8716,** Election To Have a Tax Year Other Than a Required Tax Year, and either attach it to Form 2553 or file it separately.

2. Check here ☐ to show that the corporation agrees to adopt or change to a tax year ending December 31 if necessary for the IRS to accept this election for S corporation status in the event the corporation is ultimately not qualified to make a section 444 election.

Part III Qualified Subchapter S Trust (QSST) Election Under Section 1361(d)(2)*

Income beneficiary's name and address	Social security number
Trust's name and address	Employer identification number

Date on which stock of the corporation was transferred to the trust (month, day, year). . . . . / /

In order for the trust named above to be a QSST and thus a qualifying shareholder of the S corporation for which this Form 2553 is filed, I hereby make the election under section 1361(d)(2). Under penalties of perjury, I certify that the trust meets the definitional requirements of section 1361(d)(3) and that all other information provided in Part III is true, correct, and complete.

_____   _____
Signature of income beneficiary or signature and title of legal representative or other qualified person making the election   Date

*Use Part III to make the QSST election only if stock of the corporation has been transferred to the trust on or before the date on which the corporation makes its election to be an S corporation. The QSST election must be made and filed separately if stock of the corporation is transferred to the trust **after** the date on which the corporation makes the S election.

Bill of Sale

The undersigned, in consideration of the receipt of _____% of the membership interest in _____, a Florida limited liability company, hereby grants, bargains, sells, transfers and delivers unto said company the following goods and chattel:

To have and to hold the same forever.

And the undersigned, their heirs, successors and administrators, covenant and warrant that they are the lawful owners of the said goods and chattels and that they are free from all encumbrances. That the undersigned have the right to sell this property and that they will warrant and defend the sale of said property against the lawful claims and demands of all persons.

IN WITNESS whereof the undersigned have executed this Bill of Sale this ____ day of _____, _____.

_____

_____

_____

This page intentionally left blank

Limited Liability Company Member-Managed Operating Agreement of

_____, LLC

THIS AGREEMENT is made effective as of _____, 2007 between the members and the company.

1. Formation. A limited liability company of the above name has been formed under the laws of the state of Florida by filing articles of organization with the secretary of state. The purpose of the business shall be to carry on any act or activity lawful under the jurisdiction in which it operates. The company may operate under a fictitious name or names as long as the company is in compliance with applicable fictitious name registration laws. The term of the company shall be perpetual or until dissolved as provided by law or by vote of the members as provided in this agreement. Upon dissolution the remaining members shall have the power to continue the operation of the company as long as necessary and allowable under state law until the winding up of the affairs of the business has been completed.

2. Members. The initial members shall be listed on Schedule A, which shall accompany and be made a part of this agreement. Additional members may be admitted to membership upon the unanimous consent of the current members. Transfer or pledge of a member's interest may not be made except upon consent of all members.

3. Contributions. The initial capital contributions shall be listed on Schedule A, which shall accompany and be made a part of this agreement. No member shall be obligated to contribute any more than the amount set forth on Schedule A unless agreed to in writing by all of the members and no member shall have any personal liability for any debt, obligation or liability of the company other than for full payment of his or her capital contribution. No member shall be entitled to interest on the capital contribution. Member voting rights shall be in proportion to the amount of their contributions.

4. Business Purpose. The company has been organized for the business purpose of

_____

5. Profit and Loss. The profits and losses of the business, and all other taxable or deductible items shall be allocated to the members according to the percentages on Schedule A, which shall accompany and be made a part of this agreement

6. Distributions. The company shall have the power to make distributions to its members in such amounts and at such intervals as a majority of the members deem appropriate according to law.

7. Management. The limited liability company shall be managed by its members listed on Schedule A. In the event of a dispute between members, final determination shall be made with a vote by the members, votes being proportioned according to capital contributions.

8. Fiduciary Duty. Each member of the company shall have a fiduciary duty to each other member and to the company to act in the best interests of the company in all dealing with and for the company

9. Registered Agent. The company shall at all times have a registered agent and registered office. The initial registered agent and registered office shall be listed on Schedule A, which shall accompany and be made a part of this agreement.

10. Assets. The assets of the company shall be registered in the legal name of the company and not in the names of the individual members.

11. Records and Accounting. The company shall keep an accurate accounting of its affairs using any method of accounting allowed by law. All members shall have a right to inspect the records during normal business hours. The members shall have the power to hire such accountants as they deem necessary or desirable.

12. Banking. The members of the company shall be authorized to set up bank accounts as in their sole discretion are deemed necessary and are authorized to execute any banking resolutions provided by the institution in which the accounts are being set up.

13. Taxes. The company shall file such tax returns as required by law. The company shall elect to be taxed as a majority of the members decide is in their best interests. The "tax matters partner," as required by the Internal Revenue Code, shall be listed on Schedule A, which shall accompany and be made a part of this agreement.

14. Separate Entity. The company is a legal entity separate from its members. No member shall have any separate liability for any debts, obligations or liability of the company except as provided in this agreement.

15. Indemnity and Exculpation. The limited liability company shall indemnify and hold harmless its members, managers, employees and agents to the fullest extent allowed by law for acts or omissions done as part of their duties to or for the company. Indemnification shall include all liabilities, expenses, attorney and accountant fees, and other costs reasonably expended. No member shall be liable to the company for acts done in good faith.

16. Meetings. The company shall have no obligation to hold annual or any other meeting, but may hold such meetings if deemed necessary or desirable. However, each member shall participate in the management and decisions of the company. When meetings are held, each member of the company shall attend. No member shall be required to take any action which would result in personal liability for that member.

17. Executive Contract. The parties desire that this agreement shall constitute an executive contract under 1 U.S.C. §365.

18. Amendment of this Agreement. This agreement may not be amended except in writing signed by all of the members.

19. Conflict of Interest. No member shall be involved with any business or undertaking which competes with the interests of the company except upon agreement in writing by all of the members.

20. Deadlock. In the event that the members cannot come to an agreement on any matter the members agree to submit the issue to mediation to be paid for by the company. In the event the mediation is unsuccessful, they agree to seek arbitration under the rules of the American Arbitration Association.

21. Dissociation of a Member. A member shall have the right to discontinue membership upon giving thirty days notice. A member shall cease to have the right to membership upon death, court-ordered incapacity, bankruptcy or expulsion. The company shall have the right to buy the interest of any dissociated member at fair market value.

22. Dissolution. The company shall dissolve upon the unanimous consent of all the members or upon any event requiring dissolution under state law. In the event of the death, bankruptcy, permanent incapacity, or withdrawal of a member the remaining members may elect to dissolve or to continue the continuation of the company.

23. General Provisions. This agreement is intended to represent the entire agreement between the parties. In the event that any party of this agreement is held to be contrary to law or unenforceable, said party shall be considered amended to comply with the law and such holding shall not affect the enforceability of other terms of this agreement. This agreement shall be binding upon the heirs, successors and assigns of the members.

24. Miscellaneous. _____

_____

_____

_____

_____

IN WITNESS whereof, the members of the limited liability company sign this agreement and adopt it as their operating agreement.

_____   _____

This page intentionally left blank

Limited Liability Company Management Operating Agreement of

_____, LLC

THIS AGREEMENT is made effective as of _____, 2006 between the members and the company.

1. Formation. A limited liability company of the above name has been formed under the laws of the state of Florida by filing articles of organization with the secretary of state. The purpose of the business shall be to carry on any act or activity lawful under the jurisdiction in which it operates. The company may operate under a fictitious name or names as long as the company is in compliance with applicable fictitious name registration laws. The term of the company shall be perpetual or until dissolved as provided by law or by vote of the members as provided in this agreement. Upon dissolution the remaining members shall have the power to continue the operation of the company as long as necessary and allowable under state law until the winding up of the affairs of the business has been completed.

2. Members. The initial members shall be listed on Schedule A, which shall accompany and be made a part of this agreement. Additional members may be admitted to membership upon the unanimous consent of the current members. Transfer or pledge of a member's interest may not be made except upon consent of all members.

3. Contributions. The initial capital contributions shall be listed on Schedule A, which shall accompany and be made a part of this agreement. No member shall be obligated to contribute any more than the amount set forth on Schedule A unless agreed to in writing by all of the members and managers and no member shall have any personal liability for any debt, obligation or liability of the company other than for full payment of his or her capital contribution. No member shall be entitled to interest on the capital contribution. Member voting rights shall be in proportion to the amount of their contributions.

4. Business Purpose. The company has been organized for the business purpose of _____.

5. Profit and Loss. The profits and losses of the business, and all other taxable or deductible items shall be allocated to the members according to the percentages on Schedule A, which shall accompany and be made a part of this agreement.

6. Distributions. The company shall have the power to make distributions to its members in such amounts and at such intervals as a majority of the members deem appropriate according to law.

7. Management. The limited liability company shall be managed by the managers listed on Schedule A, which shall accompany and be made a part of this agreement. These managers may or may not be members of the company and each manager shall have an equal vote with other managers as to management decisions. Managers shall serve until resignation or death or until they are removed by a majority vote of the members. Replacement managers shall be selected by a majority vote of the members. Managers shall have no personal liability for expenses, obligations or liabilities of the company.

8. Fiduciary Duty. Each member of the company shall have a fiduciary duty to each other member and to the company to act in the best interests of the company in all dealing with and for the company.

9. Registered Agent. The company shall at all times have a registered agent and registered office. The initial registered agent and registered office shall be listed on Schedule A, which shall accompany and be made a part of this agreement.

10. Assets. The assets of the company shall be registered in the legal name of the company and not in the names of the individual members.

11. Records and Accounting. The company shall keep an accurate accounting of its affairs using any method of accounting allowed by law. All members shall have a right to inspect the records during normal business hours. The members shall have the power to hire such accountants as they deem necessary or desirable.

12. Banking. The members of the company shall be authorized to set up bank accounts as in their sole discretion are deemed necessary and are authorized to execute any banking resolutions provided by the institution in which the accounts are being set up.

13. Taxes. The company shall file such tax returns as required by law. The company shall elect to be taxed as a majority of the members decide is in their best interests. The "tax matters partner," as required by the Internal Revenue Code, shall be listed on Schedule A, which shall accompany and be made a part of this agreement.

14. Separate Entity. The company is a legal entity separate from its members. No member shall have any separate liability for any debts, obligations or liability of the company except as provided in this agreement.

15. Indemnity and Exculpation. The limited liability company shall indemnify and hold harmless its members, managers, employees and agents to the fullest extent allowed by law for acts or omissions done as part of their duties to or for the company. Indemnification shall include all liabilities, expenses, attorney and accountant fees, and other costs reasonably expended. No member shall be liable to the company for acts done in good faith.

16. Meetings. The company shall have no obligation to hold annual or any other meeting, but may hold such meetings if deemed necessary or desirable. However, each member shall participate in the management and decisions of the company. When meetings are held, each member of the company shall attend.

No member shall be required to take any action which would result in personal liability for that member.

17. Executive Contract. The parties desire that this agreement shall constitute an executive contract under 1 U.S.C. §365.

18. Amendment of this Agreement. This agreement may not be amended except in writing signed by all of the members.

19. Conflict of Interest. No member shall be involved with any business or undertaking which competes with the interests of the company except upon agreement in writing by all of the members.

20. Deadlock. In the event that the members cannot come to an agreement on any matter the members agree to submit the issue to mediation to be paid for by the company. In the event the mediation is unsuccessful, they agree to seek arbitration under the rules of the American Arbitration Association.

21. Dissociation of a Member. A member shall have the right to discontinue membership upon giving thirty days notice. A member shall cease to have the right to membership upon death, court-ordered incapacity, bankruptcy or expulsion. The company shall have the right to buy the interest of any dissociated member at fair market value.

22. Dissolution. The company shall dissolve upon the unanimous consent of all the members or upon any event requiring dissolution under state law. In the event of the death, bankruptcy, permanent incapacity, or withdrawal of a member the remaining members may elect to dissolve or to continue the continuation of the company.

23. General Provisions. This agreement is intended to represent the entire agreement between the parties. In the event that any party of this agreement is held to be contrary to law or unenforceable, said party shall be considered amended to comply with the law and such holding shall not affect the enforceability of other terms of this agreement. This agreement shall be binding upon the heirs, successors and assigns of the members.

24. Miscellaneous. _____

_____

_____

_____

_____

IN WITNESS whereof, the members of the limited liability company sign this agreement and adopt it as their operating agreement.

_____   _____

_____   _____

The undersigned accepts the position of manager and all of the responsibilities and duties thereof.
_____

_____, Manager

Schedule A to
Limited Liability Company
Operating or Management Agreement of

_____

1. **Initial member(s):** The initial member(s) are:

2. **Capital Contribution(s):** The capital contribution(s) of the member(s) is/are:

3. **Profits and Losses:** The profits, losses and other tax matters shall be allocated among the members in the following percentages:

4. **Management:** The company shall be managed by:

5. **Registered Agent:** The initial registered agent and registered office of the company are:

6. **Tax Matters:** The tax matters partner is:

This page intentionally left blank

Minutes of a Meeting of Members of

_____

A meeting of the members of the company was held on _____, at
_____.

The following were present, being all the members of the limited liability company:

_____   _____

_____   _____

_____   _____

The meeting was called to order and it was moved, seconded and unanimously carried that
_____ act as Chairman and that _____ act as
Secretary.

After discussion and upon motion duly made, seconded and carried the following resolution(s)
were adopted:

There being no further business to come before the meeting, upon motion duly made, seconded
and unanimously carried, it was adjourned.

_____
Secretary

Members:

_____

_____

_____

This page intentionally left blank

Certificate of Authority

for

_____

This is to certify that the above limited liability company is managed by its

☐ members

☐ managers

who are listed below and that each of them is authorized and empowered to transact business on behalf of the company.

Name

Address

_____   _____

_____

_____   _____

_____

_____   _____

_____   _____

Date: _____

Name of company:

_____

By: _____

Position: _____

This page intentionally left blank

Banking Resolution of

_____

The undersigned, being a member of the above limited liability company authorized to sign this resolution, hereby certifies that on the _____ day of _____, 20_____ the members of the limited liability company adopted the following resolution:

RESOLVED that the limited liability company open bank accounts with _____ and that the members of the company are authorized to take such action as is necessary to open such accounts; that the bank's printed form of resolution is hereby adopted and incorporated into these minutes by reference; that any _____ of the following person(s) shall have signature authority over the account:

_____   _____

_____   _____

and that said resolution has not been modified or rescinded.

Date: _____

_____
Authorized member

This page intentionally left blank

ARTICLES OF CORRECTION
FOR
FLORIDA OR FOREIGN LIMITED LIABILITY COMPANY

Pursuant to section 608.4115, F.S., this document is being submitted **within the required 30 business days** to correct the **attached** articles of organization or application to transact business in Florida.

FIRST: The name of the limited liability company is:

_____

SECOND: The articles of organization or the application to transact business

(CHECK THE APPROPRIATE BOX AND COMPLETE THE APPLICABLE STATEMENT

☐   Contains an incorrect statement. The incorrect statement, the reason the statement is incorrect, and the corrected statement are as follows:

_____

_____

_____

_____

OR

☐   Was defectively signed. The manner in which the document was defectively signed and the appropriate correction are as follows:

_____

_____

_____

_____

Dated: _____, _____.

_____
Signature of a member or authorized representative of a member

_____
Typed or printed name of signee

Filing Fee: **$25.00**
Certified Copy: **$30.00 (optional)**

CR2E062 (08/05)

This page intentionally left blank

ARTICLES OF AMENDMENT
TO
ARTICLES OF ORGANIZATION
OF

_____

(Present Name)
(A Florida Limited Liability Company)

FIRST: The Articles of Organization were filed on _____ and assigned
document number _____.

SECOND: This amendment is submitted to amend the following:

_____

_____

_____

_____

_____

_____

_____

_____

_____

_____

_____

_____

Dated _____ , _____ .

_____

Signature of a member or authorized representative of a member

_____

Typed or printed name of signee

Filing Fee: $25.00

This page intentionally left blank

STATEMENT OF CHANGE OF REGISTERED OFFICE OR REGISTERED AGENT OR BOTH FOR LIMITED LIABILITY COMPANY

Pursuant to the provisions of sections 608.416 or 608.508, Florida Statutes, the undersigned limited liability company submits the following statement in order to change its registered office or registered agent, or both, in the State of Florida.

1. The name of the limited liability company is: _____

2. The mailing address of the limited liability company is : _____

_____

_____ _____
3. Date of filing/registration in Florida   4. Document number

5. The name of the registered agent and the registered office address as shown on the records of the Florida Department of State:

_____
Name

_____
Address

_____
City, State and Zip

6. The name and address of the new registered agent and/or office:

_____
Name

_____
Florida street address (P.O. Box **NOT** acceptable)

_____FL_____
City, State and Zip

If the limited liability company is not organized under the laws of the State of Florida, it is hereby confirmed that after the change or changes are made, the Florida street address of the registered office and the business office of the registered agent will be identical. Or, in the case of a Florida limited liability company, it is hereby confirmed that the change(s) was/were authorized by an affirmative vote of the members of the limited liability company or as otherwise provided in the articles of organization or the operating agreement of the limited liability company.

_____
(Signature of a member or authorized representative of a member)

_____
(Printed or typed name of signee)

I hereby accept the appointment as registered agent and agree to act in this capacity. I further agree to comply with the provisions of all statutes relative to the proper and complete performance of my duties, and I am familiar with and accept the obligations of my position as registered agent as provided for in Chapter 608, F.S. Or, if this document is being filed to merely reflect a change in the registered office address, I hereby confirm that the limited liability company has been notified in writing of this change.

_____
(Signature of Registered Agent)

Division of Corporations, P.O. Box 6327, Tallahassee, FL 32314
FILING FEE: $25.00

INHS18 (8/05)

This page intentionally left blank

RESIGNATION OF REGISTERED AGENT FOR A LIMITED LIABILITY COMPANY

Pursuant to the provisions of section 608.416(2) or 608.509, Florida Statutes, the undersigned,

_____ , hereby resigns as
(Name of Registered Agent)

Registered Agent for _____

_____
(Name of Limited Liability Company)

_____
(Document Number, if known)

A copy of this resignation was mailed to the above listed limited liability company at its last known address.

The agency is terminated and the office discontinued on the 31st day after the date on which this statement is filed.

_____
(Signature of Resigning Agent)

If signing on behalf of an entity:

_____
(Typed or Printed Name)

_____
(Capacity)

FILING FEES:
$ 85.00   Active limited liability company
$ 25.00   Administratively dissolved/ voluntarily dissolved/
            withdrawn limited liability company

Make checks payable to Florida Department of State and mail to:
Division of Corporations
P.O. Box 6327
Tallahassee, FL 32314

INHS17 (08/05)

This page intentionally left blank

RESIGNATION OF MEMBER, MANAGING MEMBER, OR MANAGER

I, _____, hereby resign as _____

(Title)

of _____ ,

(Limited Liability Company)

a limited liability company organized under the laws of the State of _____ ,

and affirm that the limited liability company has been notified in writing of the resignation.

_____

(Signature of resigning manager, managing member or member)

FILING FEE IS $25.00

Make checks payable to Florida Department of State and mail to:
Division of Corporations
P.O. Box 6327
Tallahassee, FL 32314

CR2E079(11/03)

This page intentionally left blank

ARTICLES OF DISSOLUTION
FOR
A LIMITED LIABILITY COMPANY

1. The name of a limited liability company is

_____.

2. The Articles of Organization were filed on _____ and assigned document number

_____.

3. The date the dissolution was approved: _____.

4. A description of occurrence that resulted in the limited liability company's dissolution pursuant to section 608.441, Florida Statutes. (copy 608.441 on back cover letter).

_____

_____

5. **CHECK ONE:**

☐ All debts, obligations and liabilities of the limited liability company have been paid or discharged.
    -OR-
☐ Adequate provision has been made for the debts, obligations and liabilities pursuant to s. 608.4421.

6. All remaining property and assets have been distributed among its members in accordance with their respective rights and interests.

7. **CHECK ONE:**

☐ There are no suits pending against the company in any court.
    -OR-
☐ Adequate provision has been made for the satisfaction of any judgment, order or decree which may be entered against it in any pending suit.

Signatures of the members having the same percentage of membership interests necessary to approve the dissolution:

Signature	Printed Name
_____	_____
_____	_____
_____	_____
_____	_____

FILING FEE: $25.00

TRANSMITTAL LETTER

TO: Registration Section
Division of Corporations

SUBJECT: _____
(Name of Limited Liability Company)

The enclosed Articles of Dissolution and fee(s) are submitted for filing.

Please return all correspondence concerning this matter to the following:

_____
(Name of Person)

_____
(Firm/Company)

_____
(Address)

_____
(City/State and Zip Code)

For further information concerning this matter, please call:

_____ at (_____) _____
(Name of Person)   (Area Code & Daytime Telephone Number)

Enclosed is a check for the following amount:

❐ $25.00 Filing Fee   ❐ $30.00 Filing Fee &   ❐ $55.00 Filing Fee &   ❐ $60.00 Filing Fee,
                              Certificate of Status   Certified Copy   Certificate of Status &
                                                             (additional copy is enclosed) Certified Copy
                                                                                            (additional copy is enclosed)

STREET ADDRESS: **MAILING ADDRESS:**
Registration Section   Registration Section
Division of Corporations   Division of Corporations
409 E. Gaines Street   P.O. Box 6327
Tallahassee, Florida 32399   Tallahassee, Florida 32314

Attached are the forms and instructions to dissolve **a Florida limited liability company.**

A limited liability company can voluntarily dissolve by filing articles of dissolution with the Division of Corporations that meet the requirements of s. 608.445, Florida Statutes, which are printed on the reverse side of this letter.

➤ Pursuant to s. 608.4081(1)(d), Florida Statutes, the document must be typed or printed and must be legible.

➤ Pursuant to s.608.409, Florida Statutes, an effective date may be specified but it must be specific, cannot be prior to the date of filing, and cannot be more than 90 days in the future.

➤ **The fees are as follows:**

> **$25.00 Filing Fee**
> **$30.00 Certified copy (optional)**
> **$5.00 Certificate of Status (optional)**

➤ Submit one check for the correct amount made payable to the Department of State. Please include a cover letter containing your telephone number and return address. A letter of acknowledgment will be issued after the dissolution has been filed.

Any further inquiries on this matter should be directed to the Registration Section by calling (850) 245-6051, or by writing Division of Corporations, P. O. Box 6327, Tallahassee, FL 32314.

NOTE: THIS FORM FOR FILING ARTICLES OF DISSOLUTION IS BASIC. EACH LIMITED LIABILITY COMPANY IS A SEPARATE ENTITY AND AS SUCH HAS SPECIFIC GOALS, NEEDS, AND REQUIREMENTS. ADDITIONAL SHEETS MAY BE ATTACHED AS REQUIRED.

THE DIVISION OF CORPORATIONS RECOMMENDS THAT ALL DOCUMENTS BE REVIEWED BY YOUR LEGAL COUNSEL. THE DIVISION IS A FILING AGENCY AND AS SUCH DOES NOT RENDER ANY LEGAL, ACCOUNTING, OR TAX ADVICE. THE PROFESSIONAL ADVICE OF YOUR LEGAL COUNSEL TO ASCERTAIN EXACT COMPLIANCE WITH ALL STATUTORY REQUIREMENTS IS STRONGLY RECOMMENDED.

CR2E048(5/04)

608.441
Dissolution.--

(1) A limited liability company organized under this chapter shall be dissolved, and the company's affairs shall be concluded, upon the first to occur of any of the following events:

(a) At the time specified in the articles of organization or operating agreement, but if no such time is set forth in the articles of organization or operating agreement, then the limited liability company shall have a perpetual existence;

(b) Upon the occurrence of events specified in the articles of organization or operating agreement;

(c) Unless otherwise provided in the articles of organization or operating agreement, upon the written consent of all of the members of the limited liability company;

(d) At any time there are no members; however, unless otherwise provided in the articles or organization or operating agreement, the limited liability company is not dissolved and is not required to be wound up if, within 90 days, or such other period as provided in the articles of organization or operating agreement, after the occurrence of the event that terminated the continued membership of the last remaining member, the personal or other legal representative of the last remaining member agrees in writing to continue the limited liability company and agrees to the admission of the personal representative of such member or its nominee or designee to the limited liability company as a member, effective as of the occurrence of the event that terminated the continued membership of the last remaining member; or

(e) The entry of an order of dissolution by a circuit court pursuant to subsection (3).

(2) So long as the limited liability company continues to have at least one remaining member, and except as otherwise provided in the articles of organization or operating agreement, the death, retirement, resignation, expulsion, bankruptcy, or dissolution of any member or the occurrence of any other event that terminates the continued membership of any member shall not cause the limited liability company to be dissolved, and upon the occurrence of any such event, the limited liability company shall be continued without dissolution.

(3) Unless otherwise provided in the articles of organization or operating agreement, on application by or for a member, the circuit court may order dissolution of a limited liability company if it is established by a preponderance of the evidence that it is not reasonably practicable to carry on the business of the limited liability company in conformity with the articles of organization or the operating agreement.

(4) Following the occurrence of any of the events specified in this section which cause the dissolution of the limited liability company, the limited liability company shall deliver articles of dissolution to the Department of State for filing.

608.445
Articles of Dissolution.—
The articles of dissolution shall set forth:

(1) The name of the limited liability company.

(2) The effective date of the limited liability company's dissolution.

(3) A description of the occurrence that resulted in the limited liability company's dissolution pursuant to s. 608.441.

(4) The fact that all debts, obligations, and liabilities of the limited liability company have been paid or discharged, or that adequate provision has been made therefor pursuant to s. 608.4421.

(5) The fact that all the remaining property and assets have been distributed among its members in accordance with their respective rights and interests.

(6) The fact that there are no suits pending against the company in any court or that adequate provision has been made for the satisfaction of any judgment, order, or decree which may be entered against it in any pending suit.

ARTICLES OF REVOCATION OF DISSOLUTION
FOR
FLORIDA LIMITED LIABILITY COMPANY

Pursuant to section 608.4411, Florida Statutes, this Florida limited liability company revokes its articles of dissolution prior to the expiration of 120 days following the effective date (or file date, if no effective date) of the articles of dissolution:

1. The name of the company is _____

2. The document number of the company is _____

3. The effective date (or file date, if no effective date) of the Articles of Dissolution filed with the Florida Department of State was

    _____

4. The revocation of dissolution was authorized in the same manner as the dissolution on _____

Signatures of the members having the same percentage membership interests necessary to approve the revocation of dissolution:

Signature   Typed or Printed Name

_____   _____

_____   _____

_____   _____

_____   _____

_____   _____

Filing Fee: $100.00

CR2E097 (8/05)

This page intentionally left blank

LIMITED LIABILITY COMPANY REINSTATEMENT

FLORIDA DEPARTMENT OF STATE
Secretary of State
DIVISION OF CORPORATIONS

DOCUMENT

1. Limited Liability Company's Name

CR2E041 (1/07)

2. Principal Office Address - No P.O. Box #	**3.** Mailing Office Address
Suite, Apt. #, etc.	Suite, Apt. #, etc.
City & State	City & State

Zip	Country	Zip	Country

4. State/Country of Formation

5. Date Organized or Qualified To Do Business in Florida

6. FEI Number ☐ Applied For ☐ Not Applicable

7. CERTIFICATE OF STATUS DESIRED ☐ **$5.00** Additional Fee required for a Certificate of Status

8. Name and Address of Current Registered Agent

Name

Street Address (P.O. Box Number is Not Acceptable)

Suite, Apt. #, Ect.

City   State **FL**   Zip Code

☐ A $100 reinstatement fee is imposed, except in circumstances which the entity did not receive the prior notices. By checking this box, you are certifying the prior notices were not received and requesting the $100 reinstatement be waived.

9. I, being appointed the registered agent of the above named limited liability company, am familiar with and accept the obligations of Chapter 608, F.S.

Signature of
Registered Agent _____   Date _____
    REGISTERED AGENT MUST SIGN

10. Names and Street Addresses of Managing Members/Managers

Titles	Name of Managing Members/Managers	Street Address of Each Managing Member/Manager	City / State / Zip

11. I certify that I am managing member/manager or the receiver or trustee empowered to execute this application as provided for in chapter 608, F.S. I further certify that when filing this reinstatement application the reason for dissolution has been eliminated, the limited liability company name satisfies the requirements of section 608.406, F.S., and that all fees owed by the limited liability company have been paid. The information indicated on this application is true and accurate, and my signature shall have the same legal effect as if made under oath.

Signature of
Managing Member/Manager _____   Date _____   Daytime Phone # _____

Typed or printed name of signing Managing Member/Manager _____

PLEASE READ ALL INSTRUCTIONS BEFORE COMPLETING THE FORM.
IF YOU NEED ASSISTANCE, PLEASE CALL THE REGISTRATION SECTION AT (850) 245-6051.

Block 1 Enter the limited liability company's document number and name. The name of the limited liability company cannot be changed by way of this application. The name may be changed by filing an amendment with our Registration Section. Please call the Registration Section at (850) 245-6051 for information on filing a name change.

Block 2 Enter the limited liability company's principal place of business address. (A post office box is not acceptable.)

Block 3 Enter the limited liability company's mailing address. (Please NOTE: All correspondence will be mailed to the mailing address of the limited liability company. Reports are not mailed to the registered office address. A post office box is acceptable.)

Block 4 Enter state or country, if other than U.S., under the laws of which entity was formed.

Block 5 Enter the date organized or qualified with this office.

Block 6 Enter your Federal Employer Identification (FEI) Number or check the appropriate box. If "APPLIED FOR" was previously reported, you must now provide the FEI number or attach a photocopy of your application for the FEI number to this form or this application will be rejected. FEI numbers are not assigned by the Division of Corporations. For assistance with FEI numbers, call the IRS at (800) 829-4933.

Block 7 Your cancelled check will be your filing acknowledgement unless a certificate of status is requested in Block 7 and an additional $5.00 is submitted to cover its fee. Certificates of status will be mailed to the limited liability company's mailing address unless accompanied by a cover letter indicating the name and address to whom the certificate should be mailed.

Block 8 Section 608.415 or 608.507, Florida Statutes, requires all foreign and domestic limited liability companies to continuously maintain a registered agent and registered office in this state. The business office of the registered agent must be the same as the registered office pursuant to section 608.415 and 608.507, Florida Statutes, and the registered office must be a Florida street address.

Block 9 The designated registered agent must indicate familiarity with Chapter 608, F.S., and acceptance of its obligations and this appointment by completing and signing Block 9. ALL REINSTATEMENTS MUST BE SIGNED BY THE REGISTERED AGENT in accordance with Section 608.4482, F.S. If the registered agent does not sign, the application will be rejected.

Block 10 Enter the name, title and street address of each manager or managing member. Use the following abbreviations: MGR = Manager; and MGRM = Managing Member. MGR - A person outside the company who will manage the company. MGRM - A person who is a member and also manages the company. Attach additional sheets if necessary.

Block 11 Block 11 must be signed by a current managing member or manager listed in Block 10 or on an attachment. If the limited liability company is in the hands of a receiver, it must be signed by the trustee or receiver.

MAKE CHECKS PAYABLE TO DEPARTMENT OF STATE.

FEES: Reinstatement Fee $100.00*

Annual Report Fee............................$ 50.00 (for each year or a part of a year dissolved)

Minimum Amount Due $150.00

* Not applicable if prior notices were not received and the box is checked on the application to indicate non-receipt.

MAILING ADDRESS:	**COURIER SERVICE ADDRESS:**	**INTERNET ADDRESS:**
Division of Corporations	Registration Section	http://www.sunbiz.org
Registration Section	Clifton Building	
P.O. Box 6327	2661 Executive Center Circle	
Tallahassee, FL 32314	Tallahassee, FL 32301	

Phone: (850) 245-6051
Hearing/Voice Impaired may call (850) 245-6096 (TDD)

Index

checks, 14, 43, 44
children, 12, 13, 19
contract, executory , 20
corporate veil, 6, 10
corporation, 1, 2, 5-10, 12-19, 27, 34, 40-
    44, 47, 55, 60
    C corporation, 1, 18, 43, 60
    S corporation, 1, 2, 6, 7, 18, 43, 60
cost. See fee
court, 3, 7, 8, 10, 14, 18, 19, 20, 24, 25, 40,
    41, 45, 47, 53, 55, 56, 66, 67
credit, 11-13, 35

D

debt, 2, 8, 9, 10, 17, 40, 47-49, 56, 59, 65,
    68
dissolution, 10, 65-68
    administrative , 65
    judicial , 67, 68
distributions, 59
dividend, 7

E

employee, 16, 42, 43
estate, 9, 11, 13, 21, 27
exemption, 1, 49-53
existence, 10, 65, 67

F

fee, 1, 6, 8, 14, 16, 17, 24, 39, 44, 60, 61,
    63, 66, 67

Florida Small Business Practice, 50

I

interests, 1, 2, 6, 7, 8, 11, 12, 13, 18, 20,
    27, 38, 44, 47, 48, 49, 50, 51, 53, 54
Internal Revenue Code (IRC), 6
Internal Revenue Service (IRS), 1, 7, 13,
    26, 42, 43, 58
Internet, 33, 34, 53, 54, 58
investment, 8, 9, 19, 49, 51, 52
investor, accredited, 52
IRS Form 2553, 7
IRS Form 8832, 42

L

license, 11, 12, 14, 35, 45, 46
Limited Liability Company Management
    Operating Agreement, 25, 55
Limited Liability Company Member-
    Managed Operating Agreement, 25, 41
LLC, foreign, 6, 23, 24
LLC, manager-managed, 23, 25
LLC, member-managed, 23, 25, 41, 55
LLC, multiple-member, 3, 21, 25, 26
LLC, professional (PLLC), 26, 27, 38
LLC, series, 24
LLC, single-member, 3, 20, 21, 23, 25, 26,
    42, 60
loan, 7, 12, 35, 47, 49, 55, 59, 60

T

tax, 1, 6, 7, 8, 11-16, 18, 21, 24-26, 40-43, 45, 47, 48, 57-60, 63
trademark, 32-34
transferability, 11
Transmittal Letter, 39
trust, 6, 19, 27

U

United States Patent and Trademark Office (USPTO), 33

Z

zoning, 45

SPHINX PUBLISHING
An Imprint of Sourcebooks, Inc.®

Additional Business Titles Might Interest You

Most Valuable Business Legal Forms You'll Ever Need, 8E

This book provides useful documentation relating to the specific structure, management, and day-to-day operation of a business. More than fifty valuable documents form the basis for this title. This new edition includes blank, tear-out forms making this title even more user friendly than in prior editions.

ISBN 978-1-57248-167-1
$21.95 US

The Law (in Plain English)® for Small Business, 2E

Every decision you make today directly impacts your future success. Understanding the many legal obligations as well as legal protections available to you is key. This book is your one-stop guide for making the right decision every time. It covers the topics that concern you the most and provides clear and accurate explanations of the laws affecting your small business.

ISBN 978-1-57248-599-0
$18.95 US

Tax Smarts for Small Business, 2E

Tax Smarts for Small Business can relieve some of the stress associated with the dreaded tax word, and answer all your questions. Its easy-to-understand format and pointed examples break down the mystery of the Internal Revenue Tax Code and give you an accessible guide for understanding the many tax rules facing small businesses.

ISBN 978-1-57248-578-5
$21.95 US

Sphinx Publishing's Florida State Titles
Up-to-Date for Your State

Child Custody, Visitation, and Support in Florida	$26.95
File for Divorce in Florida Without Children	$24.95
File for Divorce in Florida, 9E	$29.95
How to Form a Partnership in Florida	$22.95
How to Make a Florida Will, 7E	$18.95
How to Win in Small Claims Court in Florida, 7E	$18.95
Incorporate in Florida, 7E	$29.95
Land Trusts in Florida, 8E	$34.95
Landlord's Rights and Duties in Florida, 10E	$24.95
Probate and Settle an Estate in Florida, 6E	$29.95
Start a Business in Florida, 8E	$29.95

All prices are subject to change. For most recent prices, please visit **www.sphinxlegal.com**.